Working smarter with IT in your business

-21st century bookkeeping, accounting and business processes

Helping businesses work more efficiently with cost effective IT solutions

Kevin Salter FCA CTA(Fellow)

Important Disclaimer

No part of this publication may be reproduced, stored in a retrieval system or transmitted in any form or by any means, electronic or mechanical or by photocopying, recording, scanning or otherwise, except as permitted under UK copyright legislation, without the prior written permission of the author and publisher.

This publication is sold on the understanding that the information provided within it is for guidance only.

Whilst every care has been taken to ensure the accuracy of the contents, the author and publisher cannot accept any responsibility for any loss occasioned to any person acting or refraining to act as a result of any statement in it.

The author and publisher make no representations or warranties with respect to the accuracy and completeness of the contents of this book and specifically disclaim any implied warranties of merchantability or fitness for any particular purpose. The advice and information contained herein may not be suitable for your situation. You should consult with a professional where appropriate. Neither the publisher or the author shall be liable for any loss of profit or any other commercial damages, including but not limited to special, incidental, consequential, or other damages.

BBS Computing Limited
30 Bear Street
Barnstaple
Devon
EX32 7DD

© BBS Computing Limited

1st UK Edition – published March 2015 by BBS Computing Limited

Acknowledgements

All trademarks and brand names and logos in this guide may be trademarks of their respective owners. Xero screenshots reproduced with permission of Xero Limited.

Illustrations/sketches © Rachel Shute
Facebook page – This girl can draw
www.thisgirlcandraw.co.uk
enquiries@thisgirlcandraw.co.uk

Because of the dynamic nature of the Internet, and web addresses or links in this publication may have changed since publication and may therefore no longer be valid.

Contents

Introduction

In running any business, there are highs and lows. There are things you really enjoy doing and things that you really hate doing. There will also be things you really excel at, and things which you find difficult. A business is sometimes run as a hobby, but primarily is run to make money to fund your lifestyle, and ultimately, retirement.

One of the tasks that often gets relegated to the bottom of the pile is the writing up of books and records – bookkeeping. Many business owners regard this as one of those chores that needs to be done every three months to file the VAT return, or once a year as the self-assessment deadline approaches.

However, up to date figures can really help you run your business better. It can identify trends, help you identify best sellers, slow moving stocks, pricing errors etc. It is no use knowing some 12-18 months or so later that the profit margins have fallen

There are literally hundreds of commercial accounting and bookkeeping packages and many businesses also run bespoke systems specially written for them. These packages will have different levels of sophistication and features. Some will be useful to a particular type of business and others will not need it. Stock control for example is not needed if you don't carry stocks.

It is not possible to cover every business type and every nuance of a business in this short publication. The intention is also not to compare accounting packages and features. Similarly, it is not possible to cover every piece of software that can be bolted on to software to provide added functionality. We highlight just a few which may appeal to a business owner (or those staff that work at the sharp end). Hopefully this will raise awareness and stimulate interest to find other tools and products which will make running your business easier, save valuable time, potentially save costs and even make bookkeeping an enjoyable experience!

This publication is therefore aimed at the businesses (and their advisers that want to know more):

- those that are still completely manual and have not made the transition to 'computerised accounting';
- those raising invoices using word processing templates;
- those still using spreadsheets for accounting;
- those that may be using "cashbook" software rather than full accounting functions;
- those that are using accounting software but are not aware of the other tools that can link in;
- those that want to find out how accounting and bookkeeping in the 21st century differs from when they may have started out.

We hope you find this publication useful and that it gives you food for thought and even encourages you to look further into some of the offerings that can revolutionise your working practices and methodologies.

We make reference to many products throughout this publication and they are mentioned as being indicative of the types of product or service that are changing the way people work. Whilst we use many of them in our own businesses, and we have clients using many of them too, you should do your own due diligence to ensure the products will work for you in your business. It is not possible to mention every type of business and every product in a particular category – this is a very fast moving space in the IT world and new products come along practically every week.

Change – the big hurdle?

There is always a challenge in running a business and that is to take the staff along with you where there are changes proposed. No one likes change. There will be some that will embrace change and others that will do their utmost to resist and put the proverbial spanner in the works to try to disrupt the changes so that the old ways are reintroduced or proposed changes do not proceed.

It is possible that staff fear for their jobs. There is no doubt they will have seen changes in methodologies in their working lives and some of these will have automated previous manual processes, to the extent that jobs may well have been lost. They may well have been one of those that had suffered and think it could happen again.

Change for the sake of change does not go down well either. There is a saying "if it ain't broke, don't fix it". However, just because something has been done in a particular way does not mean it is the most efficient or best method. The "thieves of time" are at work….eating into the working day. Yes, there are jobs which, when complete, may provide a sense of purpose and achievement, but there are other jobs and tasks which are simply mundane and laborious. An example; a change of programs which necessitates transferring information from one product to another. The laborious and mundane way is simply to sit there day after day rekeying all the data into the new product. But is there any job satisfaction in this?

Another common, often heard phrase, when challenging a method or procedure is "that is the way we have always done it". These procedures may not have changed despite the introduction of other technologies. A simple example – a procedure was always to send a remittance advice with a cheque payment. Despite moving to the payment of suppliers online through the bank, a remittance slip was still printed and posted. The software allowed remittance advices to be emailed but this had not been invoked. "We always post out remittance advices".

The third commonly heard phrase is "It does not take very long...." and this is potentially the biggest thief of time.. It may come about simply because no one knows there is a better and more efficient way of working.

What time scale are we talking about here in terms of length?

It may appear to take seconds each time. A classic example is the logging into a web page or a program. This will more than likely require a user login and a password. This might be short and sweet or it could be 40-60 characters of typing required. It may take say 30 seconds to type all the information – it does not take long. But what about the occasions where you access an infrequently used product or web page and you have to go and look up the login details. It will take considerably longer then. What if you are logging in and out of the program at various intervals during the day? Go in 10 times a day and that is 5 minutes wasted- 25 minutes a week, 1200 minutes a year – 20 hours in total.

Even if something takes just an hour or so a week, over the course of a year it may be possible to save at least a week's work (40-50 hours) by doing it differently and more efficiently.

Multiply this saving across several different tasks and you may well find that you do not need to incur the expense of employing another member of staff or you can take a few extra days off!

It is often the case that owner managers do not get involved with every aspect of the business and really are not fully aware of how things are done and what procedures are in place. Staff are employed to take care of these functions such as the accounting, sales, marketing etc. leaving the business owner to do other things.

It is no different in an accounting practice, which is a business too. There is often a payroll department and this processes payrolls, files RTI (real time information) returns and sends out payslips to the client. However, a "deep dive" into how the processing is being done, how output is supplied (or how it could be supplied) and how and which reports are distributed can sometimes be an eye opener. We will consider this in more detail later on.

This idea of a "deep dive" review can be done internally but often there is merit in bringing in an outside consultant to discuss and review the practices and procedures.

I would recommend you ask someone "How long does it take to do…..". I would be willing to hazard a guess that 9 times out of 10 you will get the answer "it does not take very long" and no one will ever say "it takes ages".

So, once again, what is the purpose of this book? Predominantly it is to look at the accounting and related functions and illustrate just some of the new technologies and methodologies available to make these tasks slicker, quicker, easier and less laborious.

What do you do now and would *like* to be able to do in an ideal world that would make your life easier?

A few thoughts as to common current methods of working – some or all of these may apply in your business:-

- Typing into the accounting records or a spreadsheet the payments and receipts that go through the bank account, and possibly doing a "bank reconciliation"
- Typing details that appear on purchase invoices into the purchase ledger
- Filing purchase and sales invoices, correspondence etc. in binders and placing into storage

- Typing sales invoices that are generated in a third party program into the main accounts software
- Sending sales invoices and/or statements by post
- Chasing people (regularly?) for outstanding unpaid invoices
- Waiting to be paid until the customer or client chooses to pay
- Marking off invoices as paid in the purchase ledger and entering the payment amount and dates and then going online and entering the amounts again in the banking system (or perhaps even writing out cheques)
- Giving employees paper payslips every week or month
- Producing management and other reports, graphs etc. by rekeying data into a spreadsheet e.g. Excel

Can we change the way any of these tasks are performed …..?

Let's investigate …………

Use of accounting software

In business, accounting records are critical. There are still many businesses that still supply their accountants with the traditional shoebox of records – probably more likely to be a carrier bag full of records these days. This consists of cheque books, paying in books and bank statements all of which need to be listed out, analysed, summarised and collated.

The next stage is a cash book where the payments and receipts may be listed and analysed. However, this is not always completed fully; standing orders and direct debits may have been omitted for instance. Generally in accounting, the bank reconciliation is key to the accounts and this is not always done in cash books. Bank reconciliation is the process of balancing what is in the cash book with the actual bank statements. These will often differ due to payments having been made or receipts paid in which have not actually cleared through the bank at the reporting date.

From there, the natural progression is a spreadsheet. This is a step in the direction of potential time saving, but this has its weaknesses as well as strengths. Whilst the columns can be set to add up and cross casts performed, the data has to be keyed into the sheets. There is still potential for error too if not configured properly. Recently for example, a spreadsheet was supplied to us with a column "paid by cash" and a column "paid from bank". However, there were actually two different bank accounts in existence and both bank accounts payments were entered in the same column, making bank reconciliation a time consuming task. This can get even messier when individual payments on the credit card are also recorded as "bank payments".

Using Excel properly and building in checks and balances and features such as data validation and naming ranges and variables to reduce or eliminate the risk of error requires a good knowledge of that product. It is unlikely that there will be "double entry" – a feature to ensure items balance in accounting software.

It is also all too easy in Excel to change information or delete items either deliberately or inadvertently. Reporting is also a potential issue. It may involve merging data from lots of spreadsheets into a master sheet, all of which can be time consuming and error-prone.

Accounting software, whilst also needing to be configured properly, can take away a lot of the potential issues that arise with spreadsheets.

A dashboard view highlighting salient information such as cash at bank (or overdraft) can be presented to you as you load up your software. There is an audit trail of who has done what and when- created, amended or even voided a transaction. A range of accounting reports are usually available as standard, including VAT returns and all the backing schedules, transactions on accounts (between custom date ranges), profit and loss accounts and balance sheets.

Choosing accounting software

There are literally hundreds of products available to choose from. These range from simple cash book style products to fully integrated systems designed for specific business sectors.

Some are free to download and use. However, these tend to be very entry level and not overly sophisticated or feature rich.

The move nowadays is to cloud based software as opposed to the traditional desktop based software. There are many advantages to this model and some of the features meet the criteria set out for this publication:-

- No time wasted in performing updates to the product – updates are all applied online and the latest version of the software is immediately available to all users
- Multi-user by default – no expensive additional user licences required
- Collaboration with your business advisers
- Accessible anywhere at any time via any internet connection

The trend to cloud based means there is the ability to link and integrate to other cloud based products and this is where there can be significant benefits as we shall explore later on.

We shall predominantly refer to **Xero** online accounting software as our accounting product throughout this publication, although many of the other products and services mentioned will work with many other accounting software products too. We will also widen the scope however to look at other business functions such as payroll aspects, document management and databases.

Xero was established in New Zealand in 2006 and has rapidly grown to become an international business. It was developed from the ground up so does not have the legacy issues of converting desktop based software to work in the cloud. The user base is growing phenomenally as it constantly innovates and moves the goalposts.

So what can Xero offer?

There are various options depending on the requirements of the business. Only available through Xero partners and not available directly via the Xero website are cash book options – without the sales and purchase ledgers for the end user. There is a non-VAT or VAT registered option.

The full system has both the sales and purchase ledger functionality and a further version has a multi-currency option.

There is little point in just listing features in each version or comparing Xero with other similar accounting or standalone products. What we will do is look at specific features that meet our criteria of saving time and removing pain points in generic functions in accounting. We will look at raising sales invoices, writing up cash books, entering purchase invoices and expenses, making payments, collecting debts and reporting. Some of these areas will also make use of third party add-on software to achieve additional functionality.

Mobile working

What we will highlight however, is the difference that working "in the cloud" can make. You are no longer tied to a PC sitting on your desktop in the office – you can work from anywhere, and can also work whilst mobile and out and about. With the app on your smartphone or tablet (e.g. iPhone, iPad etc.) you have your accounting information at your fingertips.

In the sample screenshots below (taken on an iPhone), you can see just a glimpse of the information sat in your hands :-

You can see your bank balances, outstanding invoices etc. You can also enter expense claims (which we will cover in more detail later on), and reconcile your bank account.

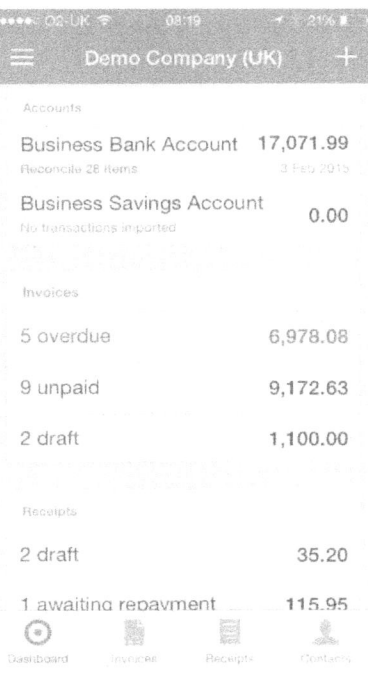

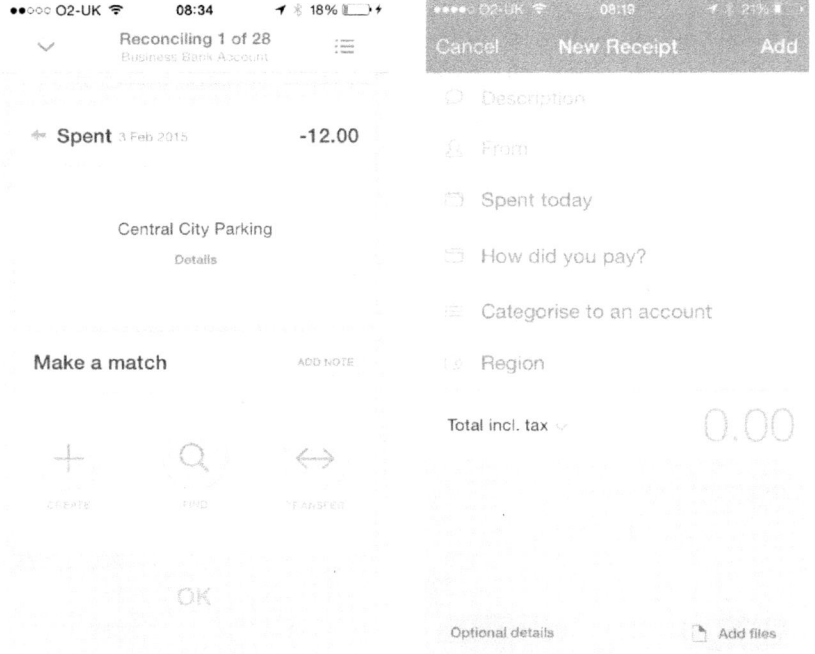

It is also possible to raise invoices from the mobile app. So if you are out at a client or customer, the invoice can be produced there and then and emailed straight to them. In the section on collecting money we will see how you can also take payment via a mobile app or device too.

Key questions and takeaways from the "Accounting software" section

How are we keeping our books and records now?	
How up to date are our records?	
Do we reconcile our cash, bank and credit card accounts on a regular basis??	
Do we know how much we are owed, how much we owe and our bank position at any time?	
Do we have key information at our fingertips via mobile devices e.g. smartphones?	
Do we present a "modern image" from our accounting functions?	
Would access to the accounting records from anywhere via a mobile device be of benefit?	
Would it be of benefit to have multiple users accessing and processing data at the same time?	
Could our data be exported and imported into another product should we choose to move?	
Do we have a suitable internet connection to consider cloud technologies?	

Automated Bank, PayPal and Credit Card Entry

One of the biggest changes in recent years in accounting software has been the ability to bring transactions straight into the software totally automatically.

It has been possible to download data from various banks in a particular format e.g. csv (comma separated value) or QIF (Quicken Interchange Format) and import the data into software. However, it was not always straightforward and manipulation of the downloaded files was often required to get it in the right format for importing. Some software required the information in two columns, some needed positive and negative numbers in one column; there was no consistency. Manipulating the data often required use of a spreadsheet such as Excel, and not everyone is comfortable using such products. Importing of transactions was seldom used to bring data into accounts software.

The method of getting bank transactions into accounts software was therefore to type in each and every entry. This often involved entry of a date, a cheque or paying in reference, the payee, some narrative describing the transaction, allocation of a VAT rate and an analysis (expense) code and entry of the amount of the transaction. There was always potential for error especially in the entry of the figures - transpositions, mistyping etc. This was not always known until the bank reconciliation was performed and the amounts in the records differed from the bank statement figure. Adjustments then had to be entered, or, as software became more sophisticated, the original transactions could be edited. Entering all of this data involves many keystrokes, especially where lengthy narrative is entered.

To reconcile the bank means agreeing the balance in the software to the bank statements. In most instances, the figures will differ as the cash book will contain transactions which have not yet cleared through the bank.

How does this change with Xero?

Bank feeds bring all the activities into Xero automatically, so that everything you see on the bank statement also appears in the accounting records – with no typing required. This is displayed on the left hand side of the screen.

It is necessary to allocate this payment or receipt and this can be entered manually as shown in the screenshot above. However, once again, there are options that can be invoked to speed up the data processing.

Create rule

A rule can be defined for both payments and receipts. This allows you to configure entries so that if an entry equals, contains or starts with certain text, it can be allocated to an expense code (or codes) based on those created rules.

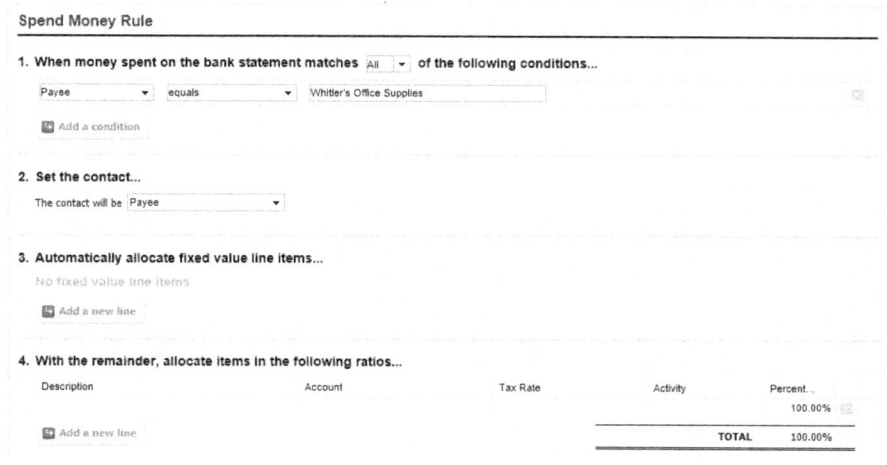

This rule runs automatically and offers this allocation the next time the criteria are matched. All that is required to make the entry into the accounting records is to click the OK button.

Automatic matching

The software will look at outstanding invoices, either purchase or sale, and try to identify a match. If it finds one, it highlights it in green. If there are several items of a similar amount, it will note the fact that there are other matches and the appropriate one can be selected. If the match is correct, again, making the entry into the accounting records is simply a case of clicking on the OK button.

In many instances, clients using Xero may have 3 or 4 pages (30 or 40 entries) imported and by clicking OK alongside all these transactions the data can be entered in a matter of just a few minutes. Compare this to the time it would take to enter all the details manually.

Cash coding

A further option is the ability to invoke an option – cash coding.

This enables the bank entries to be sorted e.g. by Payee as shown above. All similar transactions can be ticked and the expense code and VAT rate can be entered just once and it will then be applied to all of the other ticked transactions.

Using this cash coding option is also a quicker way of reconciling transactions rather than clicking on OK each time as above. We will see examples of this shortly.

Video link - Set up bank feeds in Xero accounting software

http://vimeo.com/91669503

Credit Cards

As well as bank imports, the software also links direct to credit card accounts, importing all of the transactions. This can be reconciled in the same way as the bank account above.

PayPal

There is also the ability to import PayPal accounts entries. This brings in all the receipts and the PayPal charges as well as payments made using PayPal.

Key questions and takeaways from the "Automated bank, PayPal and Credit card entry" section

Are we still manually keying bank, PayPal and/or credit card transactions?	
Could/should we import files downloaded from the bank to avoid rekeying?	
Could/should we implement automatic bank, PayPal or credit card feeds to save rekeying?	
Could/should we use the bank rules feature to automatically code regular transactions?	
Could/should we use cash coding to speed up data entry in Xero?	
Could/may we possibly actually enjoy interacting with the software? (Yes – people do say they now enjoy bookkeeping!)	

Raising and sending quotes and sales invoices

Many businesses raise invoices for their sales of products or services. As with anything accounting related, this has the potential to be time consuming and error prone e.g. incorrect pricing. There are various things that can be done to make this process quicker and easier and we will once again explore the features in Xero that can free up time and make the process smoother.

Product Codes

A feature of invoicing or quoting for products or services is the description of the item being sold. There may be a particular product type that has many variations e.g. different colours or sizes. When providing a service, the same text may be used each time e.g. Boiler maintenance for 12 months. It will save time if as little text as possible can be entered to bring up the full text on the invoice - so our product code for the example here could be PM-BR, Typing just the first two letters (or selecting it from the dropdown list) and tabbing to the next field will add that text along with the pricing and default posting code for the sale.

Example – set up inventory code PM-BR as follows:-

Sales

Unit Price	250.00
Account	200 - Sales
Tax Rate	20% (VAT on Income)
Description	Project management & implementation - branding workshop with your team

The item can be selected from the drop down menu when raising a sales invoice or quotation.

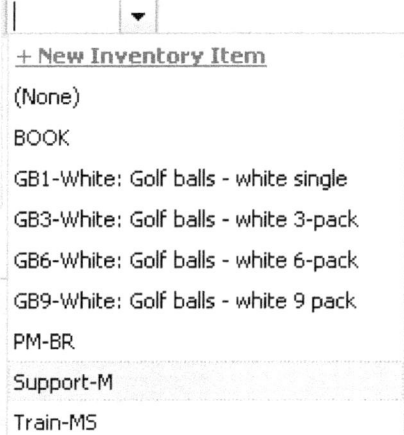

Selecting PM-BR from the dropdown list produces:-

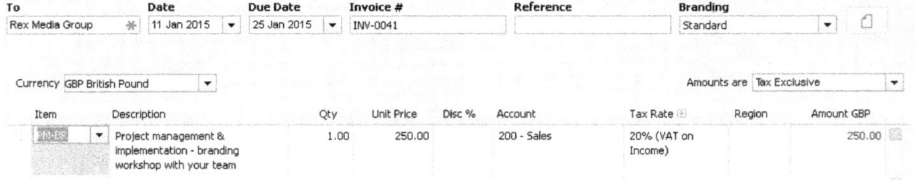

Quotes

The starting point for many businesses in the sales process is the preparation of quotes. There are various add-on products that link with Xero but introduced into Xero itself in January 2015 is the first release of the quotes system. There are further enhancements promised down the line.

A new quote can be created from the Sales dashboard and an overview of all quotes created is available.

Quotes See all

Draft	Sent (1)	Accepted	Expired
None	38.40	None	None

Once a quote is accepted, it can be converted to an invoice with a couple of clicks. As we shall consider in more detail shortly, the use of email to distribute these quotes is a) cost effective and b) a practically instant method of delivery.

By clicking on the various types it is possible to see the quotes that have been sent, accepted or expired, and in another screen, the quotes that have been invoiced out.

Video link – Quotes in Xero

http://youtu.be/39IB1Kmt5Dk

Automated invoicing

If you raise regular invoices on a recurring basis, Xero can automate this for you. There are many businesses where this is a common requirement. A few examples are listed – these could be monthly, quarterly, six monthly, annually:-

- Membership subscriptions or fees
- Software support fees
- Maintenance contracts e.g. for alarm systems or gas servicing
- Retainer fees

The invoices can be either draft, needing to be reviewed or edited prior to issue or can be posted direct. They can also be emailed out to the customers without any intervention whatsoever.

Why use recurring invoices?

By setting an invoice as recurring, it will pop up every time at the selected interval so there is no danger of it being forgotten or overlooked. It can also be set so that the price is automatically entered too if this is unlikely to change on each occurrence. These invoices can be viewed first or can be set to be automatically sent out. Once accepted, the sales ledger is obviously automatically updated.

Video link - This video tutorial shows you how to create repeating invoices and bills in Xero accounting software.

http://vimeo.com/76367186

Distribution of quotes and invoices

The traditional method of distributing invoices is to print them out, one copy for the customer and (at least) one copy to place on a file. The invoices are then placed in envelopes and posted out. First class or second class postage? Whichever option is chosen, the costs can soon mount up and this can be a laborious manual process. There will also be a delay in them landing on the relevant desk for processing and passing for payment.

Consideration should be given to sending the invoices electronically. A simple method is by email, usually in a PDF (portable document format) so that it can be opened on practically any device.

Using email avoids the cost of postal mailing and ensures the invoice is dispatched as soon as practicably possible after being raised. This applies to any business of any type, and is not just sending to other businesses; it applies equally to individuals too. Granted not everyone in business or personally is comfortable using email so it will probably not be possible in all cases, but it will work for many. There will be businesses that would actually prefer to receive it electronically as we shall see in the Purchase invoices section. The local milkman sends his invoices as a PDF attached to an email-why shouldn't your business do it? Do you ask all customers how they would like to receive their bills?

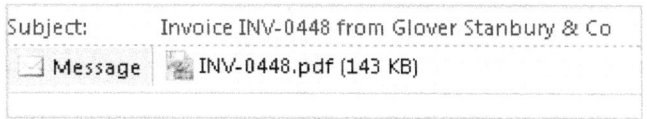

PDF Invoice attached to an email

A further option that exists where both the seller and purchaser use Xero is the ability to send invoices internally via the Xero network. Each Xero organisation has a unique and private network key. If you want to send an organisation invoices from Xero to Xero, you'll need to ask them for their network key.

When an organisation that has your key sends you a Xero to Xero sales invoice, you'll receive it as a draft bill. You'll need to choose the account and tracking for the bill before it can be entered into Xero but all other information is automatically populated.

Key questions and takeaways from the "Raising and sending sales invoices" section

How do we produce and issue quotes now? (handwritten, word processed….?)	
How do we produce and issue invoices now? (handwritten, word processed….?)	
Could/should we consider using "product codes" to simplify the entry of standard text/products on invoices?	
Could/should we consider the use of "recurring invoices" for regular billings?	
Could we ask customers whether they would like invoices sent via email instead of by post?	
Could we obtain their email address before we need to send invoices out?	
Could/should we consider sending invoices to customers that use Xero via the Xero to Xero network?	

Collecting the money

Having raised invoices, or just selling in general, the next stage Is to ensure the monies are collected in promptly. "Cash is King" is the well-known saying. The key is to make it as easy as possible for clients or customers to pay.

Bills sent via post are probably put in a pile along with all the others and will be paid in the monthly pay run if the business is sufficiently organised. In other cases however, the debtors may take as long as they possibly can before paying you. If you email bills, there is a possibility that this may be actioned sooner, especially if it can be paid with a couple of clicks.

Pay direct to bank

Do you make sure the client or customer is aware of your bank details – sort code and account number? Are they printed on the bottom of your invoices? What about statements? There are advantages in having it paid directly into the account:-

- This can save cost as direct credits often incur cheaper bank charges than cheque processing,
- The funds are likely to be available to you much more quickly – both in terms of the time taken for funds to "clear" and delays in getting cheques taken to the bank – both in reaching you via the post and in actually taking them to the bank; "it's only a couple of small cheques-not worth banking yet-I'll wait for some more to come in".

Credit cards

Credit cards are now the most common method of payment, regardless of the industry. Accepting cards may mean payments to the bank are delayed to a degree, and there are usually processing charges and fees associated.

Setting up credit card facilities requires a merchant service provider-essentially an intermediary between the credit card and your bank account. These intermediaries process the information, collect funds and then transfer the monies into your bank account.

Merchant providers historically have been your own banks, but there are now many others offering such a service.

Many businesses will take credit cards and make the customer aware. Something similar to this may appear on invoices, statements etc.

However, to make payment usually means having to telephone so that the payment can be processed manually via the card machine. This is not convenient for those trying to pay at 8 o'clock in the evening. Consider having a link on your website or a live link on invoices sent electronically to accept credit card payments 24/7/365.

For the purpose of this section we will consider eWAY. To set up eWAY requires online registration or it can be done over the telephone. A connection is set up with your selected bank. eWAY supports over 60 shopping carts so you should be able to link to one that fulfills your need for an online store. You can also place a link on your website to accept credit card payments 24/7/365 for other types of business or trade e.g. plumbers, electricians etc.

Mobile credit cards

A feature of eWAY is the mobile app allowing you to process credit cards on smartphones and tablet devices. An internet connection is required however.

When sending invoices via Xero, the eWAY add-in PayThis makes it easy for people to pay you. It is possible to add live links to your invoices which allow the recipient to click and be taken to a web page where they can pay immediately by debit or credit card. You do not need to be using credit card payment facilities already; it can all be done online. Indeed, you may choose to not have a physical credit card terminal completely and have a link on your website where payments can be entered.

The invoice will appear with payment links similar to that shown below.

Subtotal	20.00
Total VAT 20%	4.00
Invoice Total GBP	24.00
Total Net Payments GBP	0.00
Amount Due GBP	**24.00**

Due Date: 01 Jan 2015

VISA MasterCard

Pay this invoice online, Pay online now

When the customer clicks on the "Pay online now" link (only possible where the invoice has been sent electronically to them) they are taken to a payment processing page where they can enter their payment details. This can also be a link to enable the customer to make payment via PayPal or to a direct debit facility (see below). The Xero integration means the invoice is marked as paid in the accounting software.

The links to paying by credit card can, as already mentioned, simply be a link on the website.

Running your business on a smartphone or tablet

An alternative and wholly mobile device is the iZettle credit card reader. You can create a product library and organise them into folders in the app. Record sales by cash and/or card and have daily summary reports in Excel format. The product now also has Xero integration so sales and payout data are seamlessly integrated into the accounting records.

The entry level chip and pin reader is available here http://bit.ly/1A5BZuh

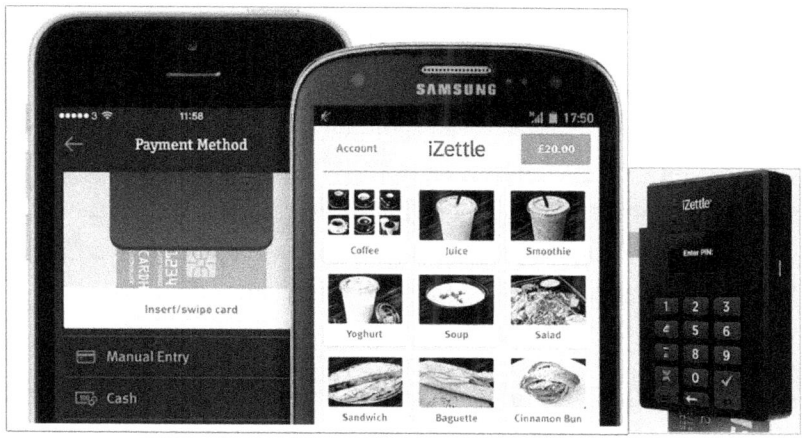

The BBC news reported in December 2013 that a "Big Issue" seller was using the above device to take money from people in the street. Are you missing a trick if you do not accept credit card payments?

Direct Debit

To get paid when you want to be paid and not when the customer or client chooses to pay you, direct debits are the best way. This used to be very time consuming and quite costly to put in place via your bank with loads of form filling before this facility was made available to you. Times have changed thanks to products such as GoCardless.

At the GoCardless website, you enter some basic information and within a very short period of time, without reference to your bank at all, you are up and running and can collect funds using direct debit. There is also no upfront cost for this service. The only costs are when funds are collected - and this is a maximum of 1% of the amount collected subject to a £2 maximum. So collect £20 and it costs you 20p, collect £100 and it costs you £2, collect anything above £100, e.g. £10,000 and it still only costs you £2.

Taking this a stage further, another add-in which uses the GoCardless engine, links into Xero. It scans the debtors' ledger on a regular basis and ascertains the due date of the invoice. It then collects the funds on the due date and it ends up in your bank account (less the 1% up to £2). The debt is automatically marked as paid and the charges are also automatically posted into Xero.

Any business that collects money (is that not *every* business and indeed organisation?) is likely to be able to benefit from implementing direct debits. Collecting by direct debit gives you the opportunity to avoid/reduce late payments. It can also cut down the significant time spent on the collection of funds - consider for example membership of a sports club, gym membership, golf club etc. How often do they need to chase for annual subscriptions?

Why not use standing orders? These need a form completed manually and sent to the bank, leading to delays in processing and setup. What happens when the amount changes e.g. the annual subscription rises by 3% - was £100 and is now £103. A standing order will collect the £100 and there may well be inordinate time and effort spent in obtaining the additional £3.

Web link to GoCardless

http://bit.ly/cardlessdd

Debt chasing

Once invoices are issued, if there is no direct debit facility in place, it is

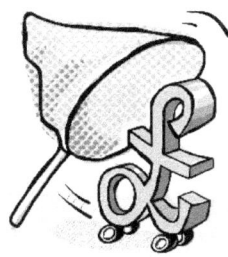

necessary to resort to the traditional method of debt chasing- that of issuing statements and chase letters, and ultimately reference to debt collectors. This has involved the printing of the statements, generation of debt chasing letters – the content of which would vary based on the age of the debt – sticking in envelopes, franking the postage or worse still, sticking on physical stamps, and placing in the post box.

On chatting to a client recently, his "pain point" - the most hated job - was chasing debts, and this is probably echoed in many thousands of other businesses around the country.

So, what other options exist?

From within Xero, it is possible to place a tick alongside either all or selected debtors and automatically email out statements showing amounts due. This does require some manual input however.

There are however automated debt chasing products. Satago is one of these. Satago easily integrates with practically any software, not just Xero. This software does not have to be cloud based; it can be used with desktop packages too, such as Sage 50.

In Xero, Satago links directly to the debtors' ledger, and, depending on the length of time the debts have been outstanding, automatically sends out a selection of chase emails and/or statements. It is possible to use the default templates to quickly set up reminders, or they can be customized by escalation level and customer. It is also possible to set on a customer by customer basis which ones are to receive reminders and/or statements. For instance, you may not want customers paying by direct debit (over which you have control of the debt collection) being sent chase letters or statements as you have overlooked the collection.

It is possible to test this product in demonstration mode so that all reminders that would be sent to your customers will be sent to your own email address.

Very few businesses actually do charge business customers compensation and interest on late payment that can be applied under UK law, possibly because this feature is not built into very much software. However, Satago calculates this and it is possible to include the late fees in any reminder emails, and optionally add it into the amounts now payable.

A Satago feature released in February 2015 was direct access to Experian credit data – free of charge with Xero and other cloud based software. It also integrates with desktop software but on a paid basis.

This access to Experian data provides: – credit rating, suggested credit limit, and days beyond terms (DBT; how many days on average they pay beyond agreed terms) – for all the customers in the sales ledger, and can easily search prospective customers before an invoice has even been raised. This data alone will give Satago users invaluable insight in to the financial health and payment behaviour of their current and prospective customers, so they can understand when (or if) they will get paid.

Once the accounting software is integrated, you can click on any customer in your sales ledger in Satago to access their credit data. You'll need to confirm the company name once to see the credit score.

Key questions and takeaways from the "Collecting money from debtors" section

Could/should we consider implementing credit cards as a method of allowing customers/clients to make payment?

Could/should we consider implementing PayPal as a method of allowing customers/clients to make payment?

Could/should we offer credit card facilities when "on the move"?

If already taking credit cards – do we need the credit card swipe machine or could it all be done "online"?

Could/should we consider putting in place direct debits as a method of customers/clients allowing us to collect payment from them?

Could/should we automatically link direct debit collection to outstanding invoices so that little or no manual intervention is needed to collect debts?

Could/should we consider emailing customer statements instead of printing and posting?

Could/should we automate the issue of debt chasing emails and/or customer statements?

Could/should we check our client's/customer's credit ratings before we do business (or further business) with them?

Cash based businesses - point of sale and stock control

 Not all businesses raise invoices for their sales. Many retail businesses will predominantly receive their income in the form of cash, cheques and credit card payments. What is important in these businesses is controlling the cash tightly and stock control. There are usually tills to record the transactions.

There are various add-ons which link into Xero (and other products) to assist in these key areas.

Vend is point of sale, inventory and customer loyalty software for retailers – again, just one of a number of similar products available in the marketplace. Vend works on various platforms e.g. PC, Mac or iPad and connects to barcode scanners, receipt printers, cash drawers etc.

Custom buttons for payment types can be configured e.g. cash, cheque, credit card, gift cards etc. You can also set it up to connect to a PayPal account to collect money that way.

As regards products, whether you sell one SKU (stock keeping unit) or thousands, you can easily manage these in Vend. You can add cost and retail prices, tags and discounts. Group products by colour or size, organise into bundles or split into units. With powerful inventory features you can see which items are in stock and the funds tied up in stock at any time, in real time.

Automated reordering can be set up based on specified stock levels and reorder points and restock levels can easily be adjusted to make sure there is never too much or too little stock sat on the shelves.

Vend and its integration with Xero

- Automatically publish daily sales totals into Xero for reconciliation with your bank account.
- Apply custom invoice branding and send regular statement balances to customer accounts.
- Publish stock orders in as accounts payable invoices to keep track of and reconcile any outstanding purchases.
- Import Xero customers and suppliers into Vend.
- Assign sales and purchases to multiple accounts in Xero to track sales by category or handle multiple tax rates.

Vend also links with many other applications – one being Shopify. Use Shopify to create your own ecommerce website. You have complete control over the look and feel of your website, from its domain name to its layout, colors and content.

Shopify Mobile makes it easy to run your business from wherever you are. Use your phone to update your store, fulfill orders or contact a customer. The data can be automatically synced between Shopify Mobile and an online store.

Here is just one example of a site created using Shopify, which is linked to Vend and to Xero for accounting.

http://www.daisypark.co.uk/

Vend video

http://youtu.be/zh2X8FyKyMI

Xero Inventory

Xero will shortly have some basic inventory features. This will work on an "average cost" basis – so buy 100 items @ £4.00 and £100 items at £3.90 and you will have 200 in stock at £790. Sell 100 of these and £395 will be transferred out to Cost of Sales leaving 100 in stock at a valuation of £395.

The stock values and transfers to Cost of Sales will automatically be updated in the accounts.

Key questions and takeaways from the "Cash sales – point of sale and stock control" section

Are we aware of our best selling products?

Are we aware of our most profitable and least profitable products?

Can we identify obsolete and /or slow moving stocks?

Do we ensure that "cut-off" is accurate as regards purchases and delivery of items and booking into stock?

Do we have accurate stock values on a regular basis to enable us to prepare management accounts?

Do we have an online shop promoting our products to the world?

Do we have tills that are compatible with or can export data to software?

Do we really need tills or can we use devices such as iPads instead?

How much work do we duplicate using existing methods and procedures?

Entering Purchase Invoices

The traditional method of entry of purchase invoices into the purchase ledger involves firstly choosing a supplier. As soon as the first couple of characters of the supplier name are entered all suppliers containing those characters will appear, the selection gradually narrowing as more items match.

The date of the invoice is entered. A due date is required which can be entered manually. However, there are shortcuts – so typing e.g. +7 enters a date 7 days after the invoice date. The credit terms can also be set up when the supplier is created so that it drives in automatically. The reference on the invoice is then entered.

An item can be selected which will fill in a description, and the quantity and unit price are entered. The expense account code or description and tax rate are then entered.

This process will be similar in any other accounting software.

New Bill

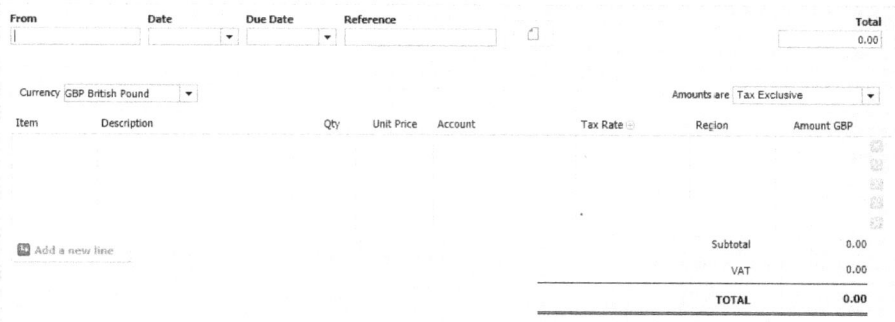

It is apparent that this could be quite a significantly time consuming process. So what other options are available?

CSV import

Provided the layout and column headings are configured correctly, it is possible to make entries into a spreadsheet and then import this file. The file layout is available as a download from within Xero.

However, this still involves typing in the data, although Excel will offer to autocomplete certain fields such as the payee based on prior entries.

Xero to Xero Integration

As we saw in the Raising sales invoices section, it is possible to send sales invoices direct to a customer from within Xero. If you are buying from another Xero user you can use this to have your side of the transaction, (the purchase), appear in Xero as a draft purchase invoice. It is necessary to choose the account and tracking for the bill before it can be posted into Xero but all other information is automatically populated.

Receipt Bank

Time to introduce a third party tool. **Receipt Bank** is just one of a number of products that work in a similar way. Receipt Bank's aim is to remove the burden that bills, receipts and invoices place on businesses. Receipt Bank has developed its software and service to make the gathering, storage and processing of bills, receipts and invoices as easy and as cost effective as possible.

Receipt Bank works with Xero as well as many other products such as Sage 50, Intuit QuickBooks, KashFlow, FreeAgent and Iris Openbooks.

In essence, invoices are sent to Receipt Bank, the data is extracted and can then be imported into your accounting system.

Submitting information

Invoices can be submitted to Receipt Bank in a variety of ways. They can be in any of the following formats:-

Jpg, png, gif, bmp, tiff, PDF or a zip file containing multiple images.

They can be submitted by email. If you receive invoices by email (which is becoming increasingly common) chances are that you (or your staff) are opening them, printing them out, posting the entries into your accounting software and then filing the paper copies. Instead, why not simply click "forward" and send the email containing the attachment straight to Receipt Bank?

The invoices can be sent by post to Receipt Bank. They scan them, so you always have them available electronically within Receipt Bank for reference at any time, and then securely destroy them.

Using a mobile device "app". There are apps available for Android and apple devices. Incredibly Simple and quick to use, just three taps is all it takes. Launch the app, take a picture and submit. No more tedious hours spent listing out receipts and analysing in spreadsheets. By doing it immediately there is no danger of losing receipts either.

Uploading direct from your computer. You can upload your invoices by clicking on the selected files or you can simply drag and drop.

Dropbox integration

Invoices can be stored in a Dropbox folder and this is regularly accessed by Receipt Bank to extract the files. We consider later in this publication a scanner which will automate the upload of scanned invoices direct to Dropbox to make this process as seamless as possible.

Video showing Dropbox integration

http://vimeo.com/35581604

PayPal integration

Any payments made via PayPal can automatically be fed through to Receipt Bank.

Processing Information

Within Receipt Bank rules can be set for suppliers. These rules include auto categorising a supplier to a particular category or nominal expense code, allocating a particular client or project to a supplier and the ability to set an invoice due date for any invoices from that supplier.

Within Receipt Bank a copy of the invoice is stored along with the details extracted. There is the ability to change some of these details if necessary and enter further narrative if required.

Exporting information

The details, once approved, can then be passed to the accounting software of choice.

These will then appear in the relevant section of the accounting software.

For cloud based software this works seamlessly. However, a further add-on is needed if you wish to export the information from Receipt Bank and import into products such as Sage 50. SageImporter for Receipt Bank will process both expense receipts and purchase invoices. The data is passed to Sage either as a purchase invoice awaiting payment or as a paid receipt.

http://www.import-web-orders.com/Receipt-Bank-Sage-50-Importer.htm

Viewing invoices in Receipt Bank

All invoices are stored within Receipt Bank and you are able to view them as and when required. You can do a search by supplier or apply a more advanced search by selecting the relevant criteria to be met.

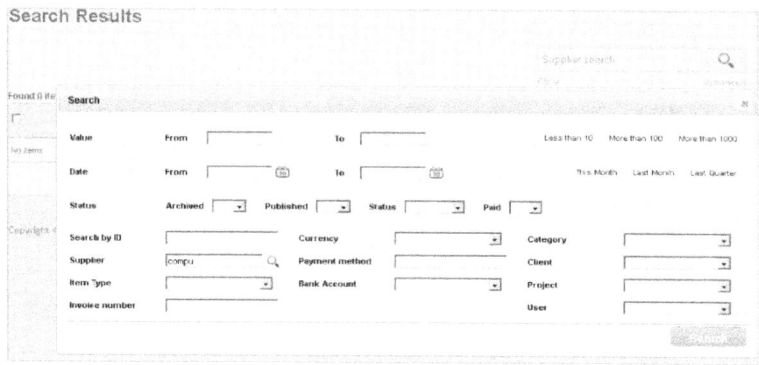

Other useful video links

Receipt Bank and Xero http://vimeo.com/106216874

Meet the Xero Add-ons – Receipt Bank http://vimeo.com/114893438

Key questions and takeaways from the "Entering purchase invoices" section

Are we manually keying in all purchase invoices into the purchase ledger?	
How long does it *really* take to enter purchase invoices into the accounting system?	
Would there be any benefit in entering the purchase invoices into a spreadsheet and then importing in bulk into the accounts software?	
Would it be of benefit to be able to see invoices directly from within the accounting system rather than have to search through filing and possibly old archives to locate them?	
Can any of our suppliers send us invoices electronically e.g. PDF instead of printed on paper?	
Where do we store files of invoices?	
How long does it take to retrieve invoices in the event of query or for reference?	
Do any of our suppliers use Xero so that we can use the Xero to Xero transfer of invoices?	
Should we consider Receipt Bank or other automation systems to reduce/avoid having to manually enter purchase invoices?	
Would taking photos of receipts and emailing them into the software be a time saver?	

Expense claims

Expense claims have many of the features of purchase invoices. Preparing expense claims can be time consuming and collating and filing receipts is also often an issue, especially when out and about a lot. From the employee's perspective a lost receipt may well mean being "out of pocket" as it may well be forgotten about when the time comes to submit the expense claims.

Xero has the ability to deal with expense claims. Expenses can be entered directly into the software through the Expense Claims data entry section. A user can be created that only has access to Expense Claims.

The expense claims are created and submitted. This can then be approved and authorised for payment. It is possible to attach receipts to the expense claims. This can be attached in a number of ways: -

- by dragging and dropping a file saved on a PC
- by emailing a file into a "file library" in Xero from where it can be selected and attached
- by uploading a file into the "file library"
- by taking a photo of the expense receipt and emailing or uploading it to the file library
- by uploading to Receipt Bank and processing as an expense

The ability to photograph receipts and immediately send them to Xero for storage in the file library prior to processing means that you can deal with all receipts immediately. As soon as you have a taxi receipt for instance, this can be uploaded instead of filling your wallet or briefcase with them and then having to spend hours summarising them into a spreadsheet the day (night!) before they are due to be reimbursed.

Processing expenses via the Xero app involves the entry of some basic information; - what is it for, who was it paid to, what date was it paid, does it need to be reimbursed etc.

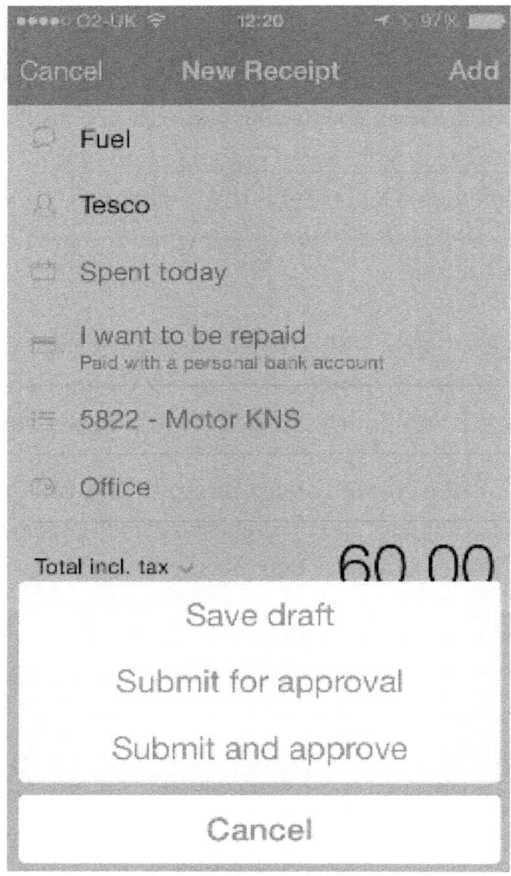

A photo of the receipt is taken and attached and this is then submitted to Xero. The ability to save as draft, submit for approval or submit and approve depends on the authorisation levels.

And here is the entry in Xero – an expense awaiting reimbursement. The photo of the receipt is also available within Xero.

Name	Date Submitted ▼	Date Due	Receipts	Amount Paid	Amount Due
Kevin Salter	25 Feb 2015		1	0.00	60.00

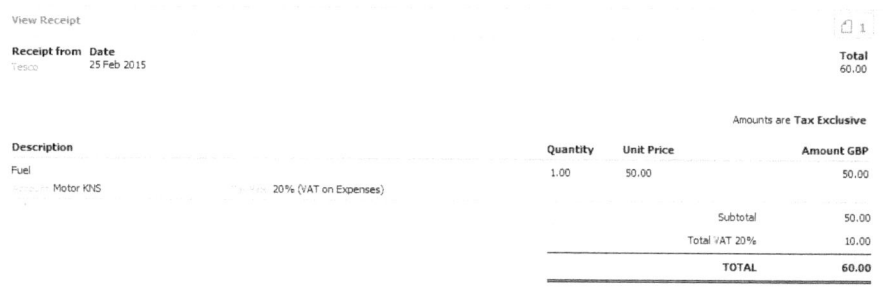

Receipt from	Date				Total
Tesco	25 Feb 2015				60.00

Amounts are **Tax Exclusive**

Description			Quantity	Unit Price	Amount GBP
Fuel			1.00	50.00	50.00
Motor KNS	20% (VAT on Expenses)				
				Subtotal	50.00
				Total VAT 20%	10.00
				TOTAL	**60.00**

There are other specific add –on products which work with Xero (and other software) for processing expense claims. We have already mentioned Receipt Bank in the Purchases section and this can equally be used for processing expenses as illustrated in the screen shot below.

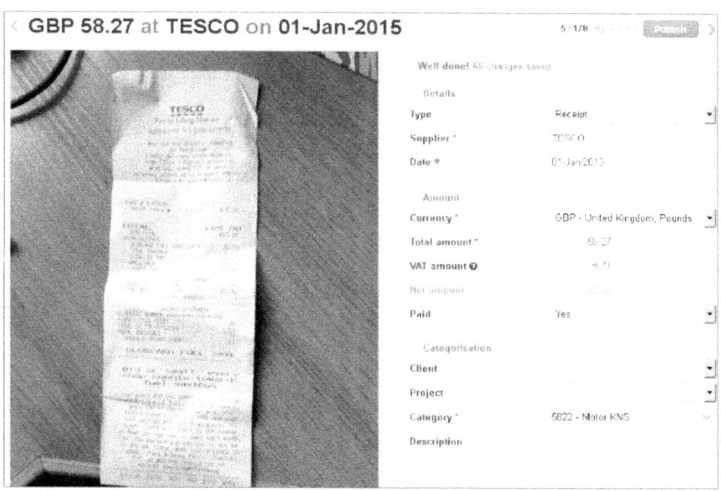

Key questions and takeaways from the "Expense claims" section

How do we process and prepare expense claims now?	
How are expense claims reviewed and approved?	
What happens to the paperwork associated with the expense claims?	
Are expense claims always complete and submitted on time for payment?	
Would taking photos of receipts and emailing them into the software be a time saver?	

Paying Suppliers

The payment of suppliers through accounting systems can often involve duplication of data . It is usually necessary to allocate a payment in the software against the various invoices that are being paid and then enter the amounts again to make the actual payment through the bank.

The most laborious method of payment is the issue of cheques, which are generally handwritten in small businesses. Every supplier needs a separate cheque written out-date, name, amount paid in words and figures and signed. They then need to be put into envelopes which need addressing. If remittance advices are printed, (which is another task), it may be possible to use window envelopes with the supplier address on the remittance advice showing through the window. Finally, these envelopes need to be stamped and taken to the post box.

An option is to make the payments electronically through online banking. This still means that the payments entered into the accounting software need to be rekeyed into the online bank, typing out the numbers twice. Again, this may "not take very long" but it is duplicating work. If there are many suppliers set up in the online banking system, it can take a while to scroll up and down the list to find the correct supplier. This is also prone to error in that figures may be entered differently in the online banking - transposition of figures, missing out entries, duplicating entries etc.

The third option is to be able to enter a batch of payments and export this batch to a computer file which can then be uploaded or imported into the bank to make the payment. If the bank does not support this, there are third party tools which may be able to do so.

There is however an option, through a third party product, to be able to enter payments in Xero and these are automatically imported into a linked online system and the payments are made by BACS. We will now see how this works in practice, and how it enables a full bookkeeping service to be provided.

The third party tool is from Credec, which revolutionises the use of BACS for making payments and we will visit this again when we deal with payroll. This is only available through a Credec business partner and you cannot subscribe for this directly.

Once the paperwork has been put in place with Credec, it is necessary to set up a "Credec Bank Account" in Xero. This is not a true bank account - it is simply the account that Credec uses and searches on for payments. Payments are listed individually as coming out of this account. The BACS payment appears as one total on the main bank account and the entry is simply an inter-bank transfer to this Credec Bank Account to set the balance to Nil.

The payment routine is no different than making a payment from any other bank or cash account. These payments are then transferred into the Credec system. These payments are viewable in Credec and they need to be authorised by an appropriate individual. Those that can authorise a payment are emailed when there are transactions that need to be approved to let them know that items are awaiting this action. This authorisation means that a full accounts payable service can easily be outsourced whilst still retaining control over the payments.

| 5 | 1,495.80 | Exported | 2014-11-25 10:26:02 | | 2014-11-26 09:43:32 | Martin Chance | View
Download |

The payments, once authorised, are paid through the BACS system. The payments can be set up to go via BACS at intervals to suit e.g. you can have for instance just one payment run a month, or one a week - say every Friday, or even daily routines.

This method of payment means that there is no duplicate keying of data, no likelihood of missing out payments and allows delegation of payments whilst still having the final approval over payments being made.

Key questions and takeaways from the "Paying suppliers (and other bills)" section

How do we pay bills and other payees at this time?	
What is involved in making payments by online banking?	
Would upload of a payment file from software for payment via BACS be of benefit instead of keying all the entries?	
How much time might we save by just entering the payments once in the accounting records and have these automatically collected from the accounting software and uploaded for BACS payment?	

Payroll

The payroll function is another area that is ripe for technology to make a big difference to the ways of working.

Xero announced a UK payroll package in February 2015 which runs payroll for the tax year 2015/16 and subsequent years. This is fully integrated into Xero. It is however not available as stand-alone payroll software and is not designed to be run as a payroll bureau service. Whilst an agent e.g. accountant, can do the payroll within Xero, there are certain factors which may influence the decision as to whether Xero is used or it is still done outside of this.

We will therefore, in this section, consider both options. Xero does promise to release frequent and regular enhancements to the product; you should be aware that this has been written based on the first release and there may be subsequent updates which change the notes here.

For the purpose of this section we will refer to MoneySoft Payroll Manager as our bureau payroll product. There are some 80-90 from which we could have chosen and there is also the HMRC online product. This HMRC product has some drawbacks and limitations however. MoneySoft does not integrate directly with Xero.

With the advent of RTI filing, it is pretty much essential to use software to be able to meet the filing requirements. This will be further reinforced with auto-enrolment and pension deductions. The traditional payroll methods are still however very much in evidence.

What are these traditional methods and what does the payroll process involve?

For each payroll run, keying in hours for every employee (or accepting the default monthly or weekly wage) is the start. Payroll software will calculate the tax and NI, any other deductions and the net pay. There may be other complications – Statutory Sick Pay, Statutory Paternity or Maternity Pay to name just two.

The payslips are then printed. Not so long ago this was on either two or three part pre-printed stationery on dot matrix printers. Nowadays, I would hazard a guess that laser printers are the predominant output device. Some payroll software products may still dictate that pre-printed paper is required. Other software may well allow output onto plain paper as an option. MoneySoft offers both options.

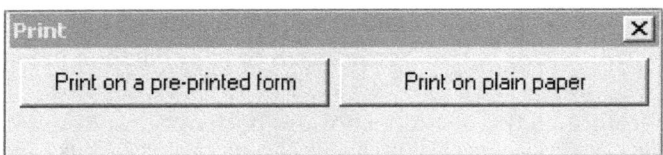

Security payslips are also still in regular use by many businesses.

Whichever option is chosen, it is a requirement that payslips are issued to staff, and these therefore need to be distributed. This may involve placing into envelopes and handing out, or in some cases actually posting out. All of these steps are labour intensive and time consuming.

Once the payroll has been run, the staff need to be paid. This can be by cash (but means obtaining the right cash breakdown of notes, coins etc.), individual cheque payments, by going online or using one of the bank systems to upload a file in a suitable format, or via BACS. We will consider this below in more detail.

Payroll data entry

Where annual salaries are paid there may be very little manual input each pay period. There may however be reimbursed expenses which are probably keyed in before running the payroll. With staff with variable hours or pay, overtime etc. there may be considerably more input however. Rekeying of data, as we all know, is always prone to error.

If possible and practicable, having the data in a spreadsheet format which can be imported into the payroll software will avoid this rekeying. MoneySoft permits import of data; Xero does not (at the time of writing).

Payslip and payroll reports distribution

How do you produce and distribute payslips? What generally happens to payslips (and envelopes etc.) in the hands of the employee? They may well check to ensure they have been paid for the expected number of hours and see how much will be paid into their bank this week or month. However, there are alternative distribution methods which the payroll software may support or third party tools can be used.

The most straightforward method which is probably available inside the payroll software is the ability to email payslips. However, this is only recommended if the payslips can be sent in a password protected format. In MoneySoft there is an option to email the files individually or send them to the employer as separate files or all in one file.

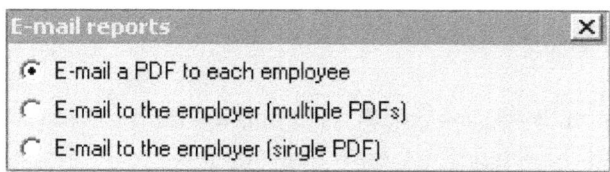

The email has a PDF attachment.

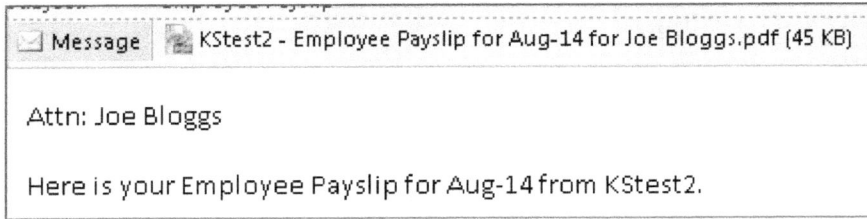

A password needs to be entered to open the attachment. Obviously the employee will need to know this or have chosen this in the first instance.

In Xero, there is an option to email or print payslips, or upload to a "portal".

Portals

A further option is to have a dedicated portal where the payslips are uploaded and the employees log in to a web page to access their payslips. There will also be a dedicated employer's view page. This methodology is available via third party suppliers as well as a handful of payroll providers. Anyone using MoneySoft would need to use one of the third party suppliers. However, the Xero payroll product does have an inbuilt portal feature. It has been designed with use on a mobile heavily to the fore. Staff are therefore able to log into their own portal from their mobile device and see all payslips.

Payroll reports

As part of the payroll process, there will be summary reports available showing totals for the period in terms of gross pay, expenses, employers NI and employees NI, tax deducted etc.

How are they produced?

Do they provide what is required?

How are they distributed to end users?

What does the end user do with them?

The payroll software may well produce a range of reports, slicing and dicing the figures in a variety of ways. But does this provide useful information, or could other reports be more useful?

The traditional method of distributing the reports has been to generate it and hit the Print button to send it to the printer and then post it out. Asking a client at a meeting what he actually did with the reports that were sent to him by post, he responded that he kept them locked away in a filing cabinet "just in case" he needed them. It transpired the payslips were being uploaded to a secure portal. A quick tweak of the methodology and these reports are now also uploaded to his secure portal from which he can download them as required.

Paying the staff

As noted above, the staff needs to be paid. Cheques are very laborious and time consuming, both from the need to produce them and from the employee's viewpoint in having to probably make a special trip to the bank to pay it into the account.

There are various reports produced by some payroll software that are in a format suitable for sending to the bank. However, some produce the reports but these are not acceptable to the banks and they still need rekeying into the online banking pages.

Another option is to use online banking directly. That phrase again – "it does not take very long" – but there are all the downsides we have mentioned at various stages before; rekeying is prone to error or omission.

We mentioned Credec in the section on paying bills, and Credec offers a solution for payroll too. The Credec Payroll Direct Credit solution effectively allows a business to outsource the complete payroll function to a third party and, on the other side of the fence, allows a payroll bureau the opportunity to offer a complete service from start to finish. It does not require any IT hardware or changes to existing payroll processes. Similarly it does not need any additional software or licenses.

A BACS report is produced from payroll software (either MoneySoft or Xero) in the required format. This file is simply uploaded to the Credec (secure) website and the payments are made using the BACS system.

A big plus of using BACS is automatic compliance with RTI filing. The BACS file contains hash codes which proves that RTI reporting has been run.

Payroll summary posting and integration into accounting records

It is common to see the net wages transactions e.g. the cheques or the bank transfers, being posted into a Wages expense account. The same posting is made when HMRC is paid, either on a quarterly or monthly basis. When running a profit and loss account however, this method does not give an accurate reflection of the actual expense for the period. This does not implement one of the standard controls that can be built into accounting records either.

Where a non-Xero payroll product is used, it is recommended that a payroll posting be made into the accounting records, which, in its simplest form can be just four lines:-

Gross Pay for the Period	2000.00	
Employers NI	200.00	
PAYE Control Account – (Tax, E'ers and E'ees NI)		800.00
Net Pay control Account		1400.00

The Employer's NI can be posted into the Wages account too or it can be to a separate account if so desired (as illustrated above). Similarly, the Tax, Employer's and Employee's NI can also be entered separately if easier. The Net Pay control is the total that will be paid out to the staff. When the payments are made from the bank or cash, they are posted to the Net Pay control. The balance on this account should then reduce to Nil at the end of each pay period-this being a control to ensure postings have been made correctly.

The balance building up on the PAYE Control account is the amount that is due to HMRC at any time. If paid monthly, the balance at the end of a prior month should be the amount paid on or around 19th of the month – again another accounting control.

The above is a simple posting – it could in fact be many lines long depending on the information required in the accounts. For example, the use of departments or branches will need separate lines. Other postings which may be needed could be pension contributions – both by the employer and the employee, staff loan advances and deductions, attachment of earnings orders and other deductions, expenses etc.

Using a non-Xero payroll product it will be necessary to do a similar posting every payroll period. Once a master Journal has been created, it can either be saved as a draft and used each time, or an existing posting can be copied and used as a "template" for subsequent data entry. It does *not* need to be entered from scratch each time.

Xero payroll will do the wages postings into Xero automatically once the payroll run has been finalised.

Xero or third party payroll? Which should you choose?

Xero	**Third party payroll**
Advantages	Advantages
Fully integrated into Xero accounting	Cost- if cost is the biggest issue, it may be cheaper to use third party payroll products
Portal option for uploading employee payslips	Can be used for bureau payroll services
Designed to be mobile friendly	
Disadvantages	Disadvantages
May be more costly than standalone third party payroll software	Not fully integrated – journal postings needed to get data into accounts software
Not designed for bureau payroll service	No portal option or another third party add-on required at extra cost

Key questions and takeaways from the "Payroll" section

How do we process payroll now?

Could we supply the information for the payroll in a more efficient manner e.g. spreadsheet for importing?

Do we receive or produce the reports and information we need?

How do we receive the reports and what do we do with them?

How are payslips currently distributed and could this be done differently?

How do we pay staff now and could we use other methods such as BACS/Credec?

How do we enter payroll transactions into the accounting records (or is it automated)?

Do we reconcile the main wages "control accounts" in our accounting records (net pay control and PAYE/NI control)?

Do we reconcile other control accounts e.g. Pension deductions/payments to pension provider?

How will we deal with Auto-enrolment?

Accounting reports and information

Accounting traditionally is based on numbers - but for many people pages and pages of figures can be very off-putting. Many suffer from "number blindness" where a mass of numbers is just totally confusing and makes it difficult to see the wood for the trees. The phrase "a picture paints a thousand words" also applies to figures, and the visualisation of the numbers by the use of graphs or charts can quickly help identify trends and issues and throw a completely new light on the financials.

Probably the most common tool for producing graphs and charts is Excel. Whilst accounting data can be exported and imported into Excel, it is highly likely that in most businesses, figures are keyed into Excel manually each time a report is required.

Whilst the Xero dashboard has some charting features, these are predominantly high level reports, and often more detailed reports are required, or the data needs to be presented in a different way.

There are various products which can link to Xero (and sometimes other software too) to give you further insights into your business.

CrunchBoards is one of these reporting tools and this allows dynamic charts to be created, with the data imported directly from Xero automatically, every 3-6 hours, so it offers a practically "real time" view of the figures. CrunchBoards reports are available to you through an add-on partner utilising this product.

A variety of charts can be created. Charts can be designed to show the data in one board at the end of a particular month or period and another board can contain information based on the current day and user defined prior periods. As many cards can be created for an enterprise as you wish to display on a board. Separate boards can be produced for different end users showing only the key data relevant to them.

The product offers real time monitoring and *email alerts* when certain criteria are met so you don't have to log in each time to constantly check the figures. If you want to know when your bank account is back in credit so you can transfer funds to deposit, or if you want to know when sales hit target in the year so you can have a staff celebration, this alert can be configured.

If you want to compare multiple organisations side by side, this can easily be done. The illustration below shows a very simple report showing inter-company accounts from two entities, and quickly and easily shows that they are equal in both businesses (as would be hoped for!).

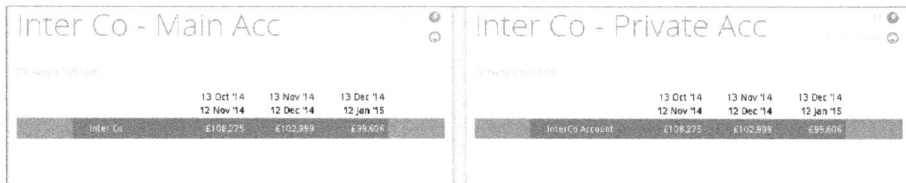

Reports can cover any time period – by week, month, quarter year etc

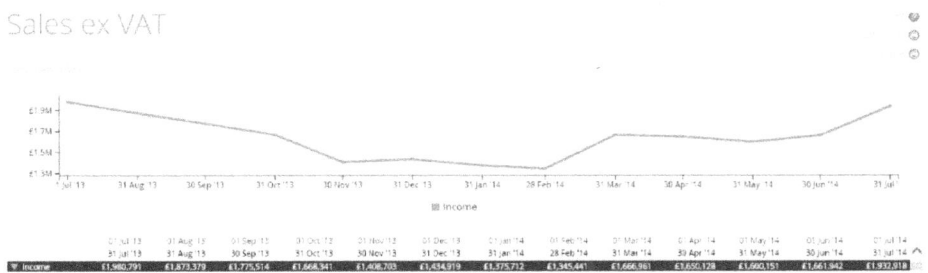

Reports that are currently generated in Excel can now be built inside of CrunchBoards using the inbuilt formula builder. This can include for

example, wages %'s, motor expenses %'s, Gross Profit and Net Profit %'s, break even analysis etc.

Snapshots

A snapshot of the position on any account at the current date can be reported.....

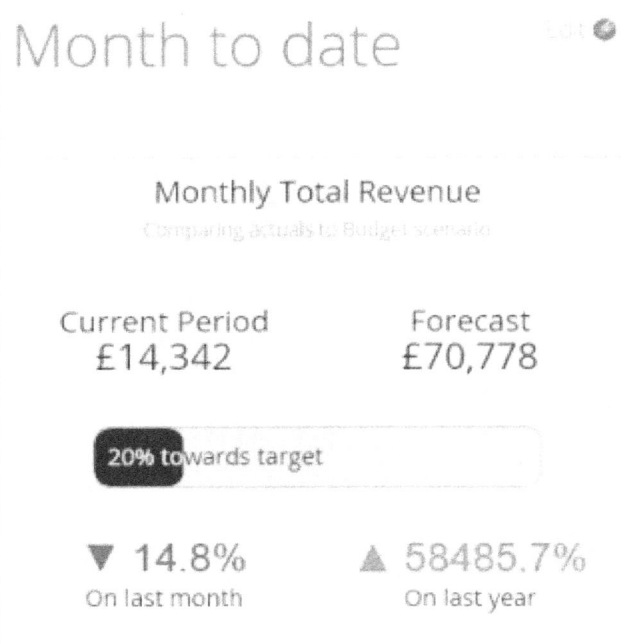

Tracking reports are also possible, where different departments are used in Xero e.g. Kitchens, bathrooms. Bedrooms or North, South, East and West.

It does not end there. When a board has been created, it can be shared with as many other users as you so wish. This creates a separate instance of it, and the user has his own control. He can manipulate the data and play with it, whilst your original remains intact. They can also share their boards back again.

Scenarios

A further option is to create scenarios – multiple "what if?" boards where the figures can be flexed and forecasts produced. This can produce both the profit and loss account and balance sheet. The manual forecasting method allows the following transaction types:

- One off transactions

- Daily repeating transactions with flexible repeating pattern option

- Weekly repeating transactions with flexible repeating pattern option

- Monthly repeating transactions with flexible repeating pattern option

- Quarterly repeating transactions with flexible repeating pattern option

- Annually repeating transactions with flexible repeating pattern option

Enter Forecast Data for: CrunchBoards Sales

✔ Test transaction

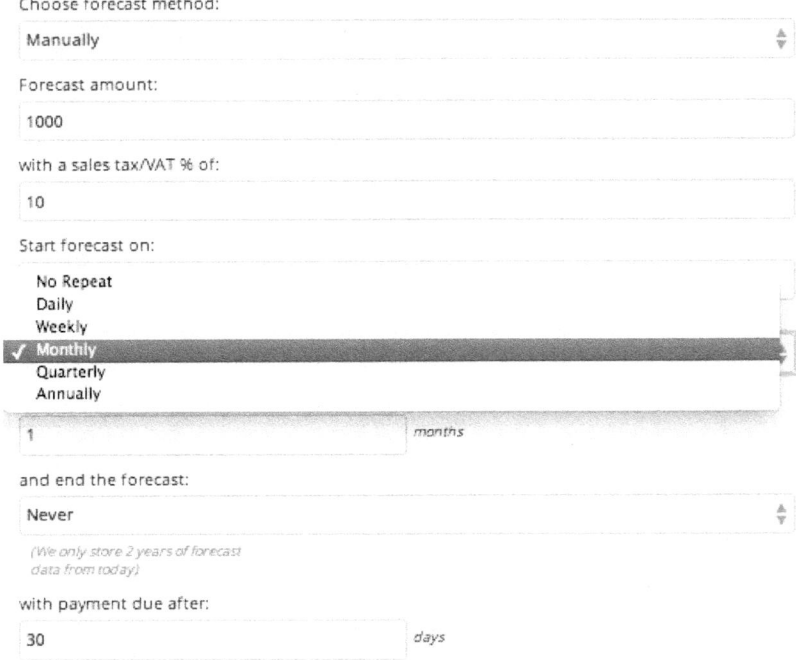

Choose forecast method:

Manually

Forecast amount:

1000

with a sales tax/VAT % of:

10

Start forecast on:

No Repeat
Daily
Weekly
✓ Monthly
Quarterly
Annually

1   months

and end the forecast:

Never

(We only store 2 years of forecast data from today)

with payment due after:

30   days

Video guides

http://vimeopro.com/crunchboards/tv/video/112368603

Key questions and takeaways from the "Reporting" section

What are the KPI's (Key performance indicators) that we need to know in our business?

How often should we monitor these KPIs? (Some may be daily, or weekly, some monthly etc.)

Do we get all the KPI's on a regular basis and how are they produced?

What reports are produced centrally and how are these distributed?

What data extraction and reports can employees run on their own systems?

Do different people need to see different KPI's?

What key events would it be useful to have monitored?

Do we produce budgets and monitor budget v actual?

Do our budgets forecast cash flows and balance sheet data too?

Workflows and time recording

WorkflowMax is a product wholly owned by Xero. This is designed for any business that needs to record time and costs against specific jobs or tasks and then invoice them out i.e. job management. There is a specific version for accountants - Xero Practice Manager - which is actually practically identical to the WorkflowMax product.

WorkflowMax is used by creative/marketing agencies, architects and designers, builders, engineers, surveyors, business consultants, IT and web services.... to name just a few.

The software has a lead manager to track sales pipeline and quotes can be produced. Timesheets are available to book time against jobs. These jobs can be tracked through user definable stages. Custom fields can be defined in the database to record any information you wish against clients or customers, contacts etc. The job management tab gives an overview of jobs due this week, next week and overdue as well as percentage complete. All your job information - notes, emails, documents - can be stored in one place.

70

Job tracking

Total	Starting Today	Due This Week	Due Next Week	Overdue
277	23	38	31	158

All   Adhoc   My   Managed By   Important Dates   Staff Allocation   Search   Archive   Recurring

The jobs on hand can be tracked through the various stages to completion
and ultimate billing. Jobs can be allocated to staff to work on and manage,
and recurring jobs ensures they appear on the jobs list when next due for
completion.

Xero integration

Sales invoices created in WorkflowMax seamlessly appear in Xero for full
accounting. Record the payment in Xero and it gets marked as paid in
WorkflowMax too.

Reporting

There is the ability to create user definable fields in the database and
determine where these appear in WorkflowMax. A comprehensive Report
Builder then allows you to produce reports easily by selecting the fields to
appear on the report, then choosing the criteria which determines what
appears and in what order, and finally who can view the report, and
whether or not they can edit the criteria.

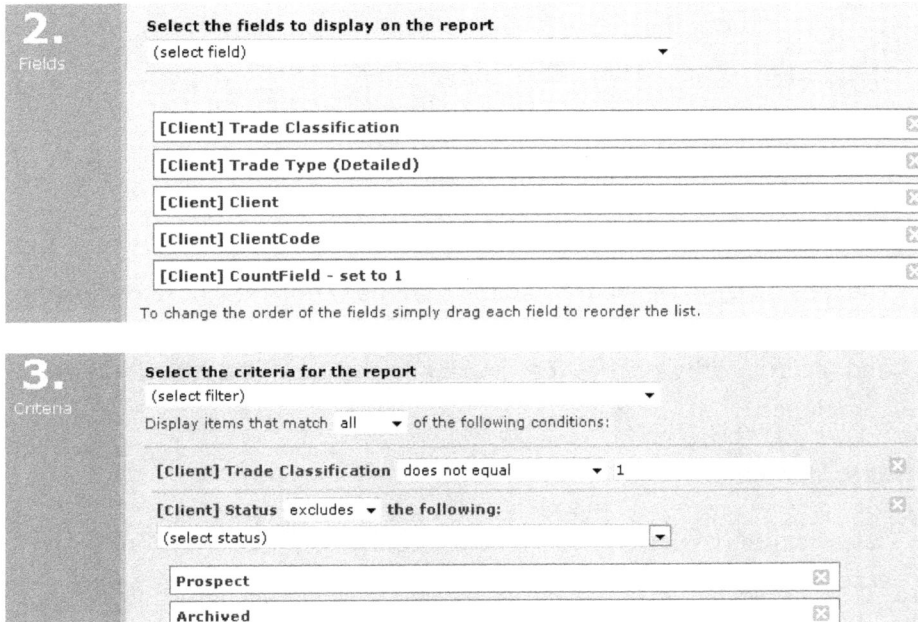

Any reports can then be flagged as "favourite" so that they appear on a drop down list when "Reports" is selected from the menu.

Video guides

http://www.WorkflowMax.com/tutorial-videos/why-WorkflowMax/why-WorkflowMax

Key questions and takeaways from the "Workflows and time recording" section

How do we record time and costs against jobs currently?	

How do we produce quotes currently?

Are we tracking and reporting on the profitability of each job? (Comparing actual costs to invoice value)

What other management reports do we need?

Are reports produced manually or are they automatically produced?

How are reports distributed to those that need to see them?

Sundry add-on products

There are many areas which impinge upon the day to day running of your business which do not always impact directly on the accounting – however there may be areas of potential overlap in respect of data. We consider a few of them here.

Online booking and scheduling software

A Google search will reveal hundreds of online booking systems and you would need to narrow it down to find one for your type of business.

However we are highlighting in this publication just a couple that integrate with Xero that are aimed at different marketplaces. The beauty of the Xero link, as with all other products we have looked at, is that data is shared seamlessly between them to avoid rekeying.

BookingBug is one such product – aimed at a diverse range of businesses such as:-

Sport and Fitness	Personal trainers, classes and courses, gyms and studios, sports pitches and facilities, fitness instructors, clubs and teams…..
Hire and Rental	Villas and cottages, B and B's, campsites, room or desk hire, venue hire, equipment hire…..
Health and Beauty	Beauty salons and spas, private medical practices, hair salons, mobiles and independents, dentists, alternative therapists……
Classes and events	Cookery, music, business, arts and crafts, dance and fitness, tours and guides, teaching and

	tutoring, ticketed events….
Service and Trade	Plumbers, gardeners, mechanics, teachers and tutors, photographers, driving instructors, electricians……..
Other business types	Recording studios, theatre booking, mobile arcades, party supply rental, entertainers, repair shop……

With BookingBug's online scheduling software you can take bookings directly from your own website to give customers a seamless booking experience.

The flexible online admin calendar allows you to view and manage your bookings and appointments, make bookings on behalf of customers, move or cancel bookings and contact your customers directly.

You can also take payments online using products such as PayPal, sagepay, and eWay to name just a few. Remind customers of their appointment by email or SMS message or use SMS to send promotions or other marketing messages.

BookingBug integrates with Xero, KashFlow and Sage One;. There are Android and iPhone apps and an iPad optimised version.

Import sales from BookingBug straight into Xero in real time. Each booking creates a separate invoice in Xero tied to a unique customer record that is tied to their email address. Any time the payment status is updated in BookingBug it can be synced to Xero to update the invoice accordingly.

Another product is **Timely**; appointment software for clinics, salons or anyone that needs scheduling. The calendar is the starting point, and this can sync with others such as Outlook calendar, iCal, Google calendar and others.

Timely will run on the Desktop PC or Mac, Laptop, Tablet or Smartphone.

Timely can handle all kinds of bookings, repeat bookings, multiple services, products, Point of Sale, stock management, staff rosters and much more. It can also handle invoicing and online payments. There is the ability to set up automated configurable text message and email reminders too.

Users include:-

Hair salons
Beauty/ massage therapists
Health clinics
Gyms and trainers
....any business that takes bookings

The Xero integration posts an invoice into Xero when you complete an appointment, applies a payment against the invoice and reconciles with the banking, and allows you to chase debtors via Xero.

Web site

http://www.gettimely.com/booking-software/tour

Video link - Timely and Xero integration on YouTube

http://youtu.be/0FNbPnWfZxk

Excel reporting and data manipulation

We looked above at reporting tools which avoided the necessity of getting data out of the accounting system and into Excel to produce the reports. However, there may be times when this is required. One such product is Excel Integration Tools. A one off payment is all that is required to purchase this product.

- Download Xero data direct from the API.
- Filters get saved with your workbook so you can easily refresh your data at a later date, reuse your reports for a different Organisation or even share it with a colleague.
- Build your own dashboards, charts and KPI reports!
- Automate the Excel Integration Tools using VBA/Macros.
- Backup your Xero data in Excel format or any of the numerous export formats it supports.
- Create Xero data sources that drive your MS Word mail merges/label printing or link your MS Access Database Application to Xero using the power of MS Office.

Excel Tools video link

https://www.youtube.com/watch?v=eZ2CB-RIaeU

Customer relationship management – CRM

CRM – customer relationship management can be a huge topic and justifies a publication in its own right. CRM and what it does can mean so many different things to different people. The Wikipedia definition is "a system for managing a company's interactions with current and future customers. It often involves using technology to organize, automate and synchronize sales, marketing, customer service, and technical support".

Xero has some basic CRM features. It is possible to add notes to any customer or supplier tab.

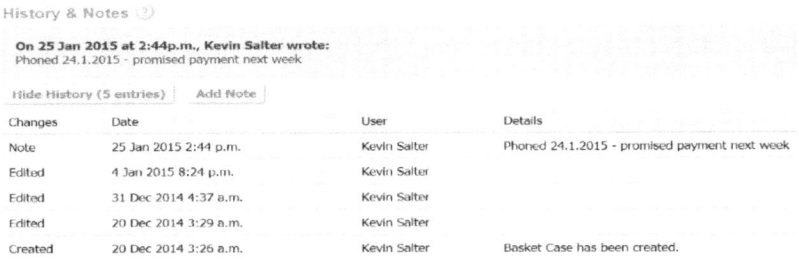

This will be available by clicking on the Show History button to expand the display and Hide History to shrink it back down.

There is also the ability to create "smart lists". With Smart Lists, you're able to communicate with organisations that are already your customers, using the data you're updating every day.

You can use Smart Lists to create a targeted list for a campaign by filtering by people who have bought a certain product, or who have been invoiced for a certain amount.

Just a few ideas of the use of Smart lists:

- Identify customers who have purchased a product from you, who may be interested in a new product you now have available.
- Find all those customers who haven't paid an invoice in the past few months, so you can follow-up with them and improve your cash flow.
- See how many customers you have in a particular city or region, helping you understand your customer base and use as the basis of a targeted marketing or sales effort.

Once you have created a list of customers you can export it to a CSV file (at which point you can do whatever they want with it, such as sending the customers an email from your email system), or directly push it to a third party email engine.

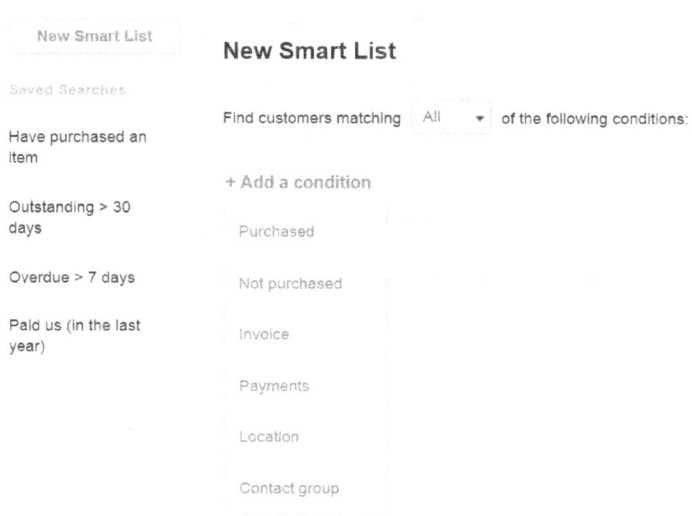

Video link

Smart lists in Xero

http://youtu.be/PXlqgvRFzd4

If you need further detail or information however, there are a variety of products that can integrate with Xero, all viewable at the Xero website. For illustrative purposes we will mention Capsule CRM and list some of the features.

You can use Capsule to keep track of the people and companies you do business with, communications with them, opportunities in the pipeline, and what needs to be done when. Combine with Xero's online accounting solution to complete the view across your invoice and accounting activities.

- Add customers and suppliers directly to Xero
- Use Capsule to easily add customers and suppliers directly to Xero as they progress from initial enquiry through to a sale.
- Keep customer and supplier records in sync
- Capsule automatically keeps customer and supplier records in Xero up-to-date with Capsule so that you only need to change them in one place.
- View invoice history and overdue items
- Capsule includes a summary of invoices and overdue amounts right inside the customer's page in Capsule to give you the full picture when you speak to them.

Video Links

Capsule and Xero integration video

http://vimeo.com/57518561

Capsule CRM intro

http://youtu.be/_7UjSdBlkzE

Other data import

It is possible that you have specialist software that you want to continue using which sits outside of your main accounting records.

This might be a sales invoicing and stock control system, a motor trade software producing other forms and records needed, or it could be a practice management system or indeed anything else. The figures produced from this software do however need to get into the main accounting records, and this can be done in a number of ways.

One way is to simply rekey all the invoices output from one system into the main accounting records. This is obviously prone to error; typing in of the numbers, possible allocation to the wrong customer etc. t can also be very time consuming (try asking the person that sits there doing this task and by now you will probably guess the response you will get – "it doesn't take very long"). A variation on this theme is copying and pasting the data.

A second way is to post the end of month totals as one monthly journal. If there is a debtors list in the external software, the end of month balance should agree to the figure in the main accounting records. If it does not, this needs to be investigated to ascertain why it does not agree.

We have seen elsewhere that it is possible to import data into Xero (and other packages) via CSV-comma separated value-files. However, even if you can extract data as a csv file, it will often need manipulation to ensure it is in the correct format for a subsequent import. It may be that columns may need to be renamed or deleted and the order possibly amended. Whilst this can be almost certainly be done in Excel, it may require some Excel competency to be able to do so. To have to do this each time there is an import required can also be time consuming.

However, there is a Xero add-on **CSV2Cloud.com**.

Web page

https://www.csv2cloud.com/

As long as the data can be extracted from one package, either as a CSV, TXT or XLS file the company should be able to have you up and running very quickly. You then simply email output files to a designated email address and the data then appears in Xero.

If this is not practicable, there may be other ways data can be transferred between products and there are some specialist "integrators" which can develop software to link them together.

Seeking Feedback

Do we know we have served a client or customer well? Or are we falling short? Is there something we could have done better or differently?

If the client or customer is not asked, it is possible they will just vote with their feet and go elsewhere. If there is an early indication that something is wrong there may be an opportunity to do something about it. It is also nice to get good feedback when something or somebody has performed well.

It is possible to automate the task of sending out feedback requests. This feedback does not need to be a huge questionnaire which is not likely to be completed. Just a couple of clicks and send should produce a greater response rate.

Customersure (www.customersure.com) offers this service of automatically sending out a short survey after purchase. Raise an invoice from your software – Xero or SageOne – and the survey is sent. It also works with Shopify to check satisfaction after every order.

Many businesses also link all the feedback (good or bad) directly onto their website so that potential customers get a completely independent review.

Key questions and takeaways from the "Sundry Add-on Products" section

What other software products do we use in our business regularly?

Does this product integrate with our accounting package?

Are there other similar products we could use which would integrate with our accounting package?

What potentially unnecessary rekeying of data could we eliminate?

Could/should we track our interactions with customers/clients?

Where do we record notes about our clients and customers and are they visible to those that need to know?

Do we really know what our customers or clients think about us?

Document Management

We have touched upon this subject, without specifically using those two words together, on numerous occasions throughout this publication. As with many of the subjects covered, we can only scratch the surface of this topic here, The author has written complete publications on document management which can be found on Amazon. We will look at the benefits and time saving features in this section.

Businesses may already store documents in an electronic format in some semblance of file structure by the use of Windows folders. So there may be a folder called "Invoices" and sub-folders for each supplier. Similarly, there may be a correspondence folder and each client or customer has a sub-folder. There may then be further sub-folders and sub folders underneath again. Whilst this may suffice initially, it will soon get unwieldy and require many clicks to drill down to the required level. Even navigating to the secondary level folder can become time consuming. There are other potential issues with the Windows folder structure. It is quite easy to drag files or even whole folders and drop them somewhere else, sometimes without even realizing it has been done. It is also possible to delete files or whole folders very easily. There is also an issue in creating folders especially if you have a sub-folder for a "year". If you have 500 clients or customers and want a 2015 folder for correspondence etc. you have to do this 500 times. This is yet another example of the "it doesn't take very long" syndrome. It may take a minute or two to drill down to the required level and create the new folder – 500 @ 2minutes = 1000 minutes = over 16 hours doing a very mundane task.

Windows folders are simply a storage mechanism and do not cater for workflows, fast and easy retrieval of data and can have a complex filing structure as we have seen. With ever increasing use of email, it is also not an ideal medium to store email correspondence.

A "proper" document management system can bring many benefits. In essence, this document management solution has to fulfill three simple functions - the storage of data, the ability to search for It when needed and retrieve it quickly when needed. The software is not in itself complex but it does require a significant change in mindset by the users. We will highlight some of the features of **Docusoft** - a specialist document management software - in discussing these areas below.

"A picture tells a thousand words" is an often heard quote and the picture below is no exception. One of the major benefits of electronic storage is there is no need to store paper anymore and the picture shows filing cabinets being removed from my office. There are 17 on the trailer, and 2 more in the van in the background. Another 4 had gone the previous week-23 in total!

Any business can make use of more space. It may mean you no longer need expensive remote storage or have to store files in your garage at home. In other cases, it may mean that rooms once used for storage can revert to offices for use or even be rented out if surplus to requirements.

No filing cabinets mean more open space and room to move around in existing offices.

Another benefit is cost savings and these come from a variety of methods. As can be seen above, there is no need to buy filing cabinets. There is no need to buy the files to put the paper in and no need to employ a filing clerk. With document management, the ability to save directly into the software and not hit the print button means savings in paper itself, as well as the ancillary costs; toners, ink, printers, other printer consumables. With electronic distribution of output, there are savings in postage costs, envelopes etc.

A third major benefit is the time savings and efficiency gains achieved. This time saving and efficiency soon becomes patently obvious. Can you deal with a query immediately when someone telephones or do you have to telephone them back a few minutes later when you have retrieved the file?

When post is scanned on opening, it is allocated immediately against the client or customer, and sits in an electronic "in tray" for both those people that need to action it and those that need to know it is there. There is no need to search around a building trying to locate a file or folder, and none of the issues that arise when it is needed and someone has taken it out of the office. For administrators, there is the ability to view others in trays to identify bottlenecks or backlogs that may be building up. For users, there is also the "dashboard" view giving and a glance view of the number of items sat in the electronic in-tray that have yet to be actioned.

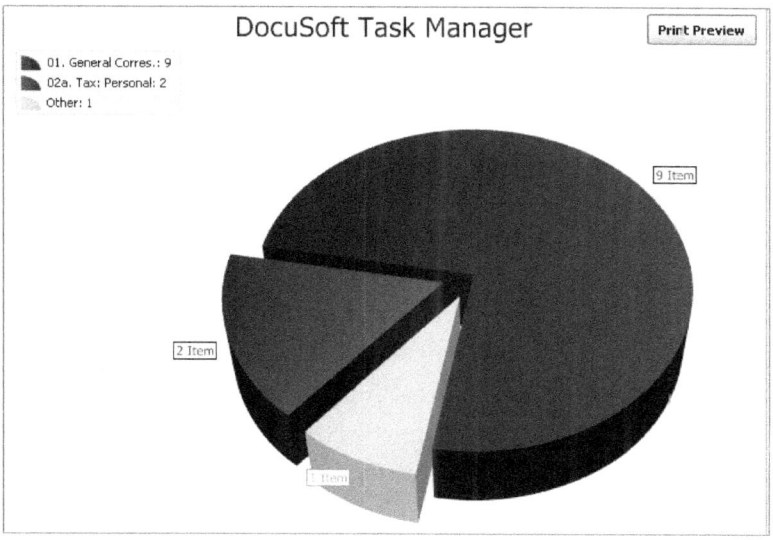

Collaboration is an increasingly heard phrase, and enabling people to work together and all have access (with the appropriate permissions) to documents is key. People may be used to perhaps placing electronic files into "shared" folders on a network, but perhaps the most problematic area with sharing of information revolves around email, both in and out. Email and email management could easily be a complete topic in its own right too. However, the major issue relates to email coming into or going out of an individual's system. Yes, they may get copied to others that need to know, but this may be sat in Outlook inboxes along with several thousand others. Some people are organised, keeping their inboxes to a minimum, or using different folders e.g. by work type or by client or customer. Others are not so organised and have thousands and thousands of emails, many totally irrelevant going back years and years. Do you really need to know that Sarah sent an email in January 2006 asking you to help celebrate her birthday and that there are cakes in the kitchen? With Docusoft and the built in integration to Outlook, emails in and out can be saved against a client or customer and are instantly available for everyone to refer to if necessary.

Saving documents

Key to the success of an implementation is having everyone on board and working in the same way.

Files of all types can be saved to the system quickly and easily. The icons indicate the type in the screenshot below. The first one below is a PDF file, the second one is an email saved directly from Outlook, the third item is a zip file containing several individual files (in this case, payslips and payroll reports for the month), and further down there are Word and Excel documents. . With Word, Excel and Outlook, there is an add-in to the main program and one click launches the data input screen to save the file to the software. There are other ways of getting data in too - right click on any file and choose the Send to Docusoft option and paper documents can be scanned and filed. There is also an option to "print" any file to Docusoft which creates a PDF file which is saved to the software.

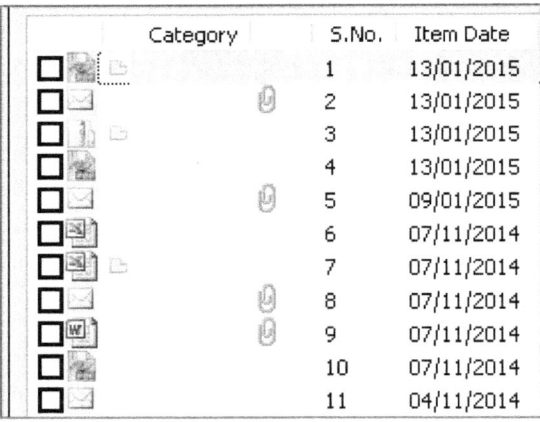

There are various columns displayed containing information related to the documents that appear in the list. Sample column headings are shown below.

Any of the columns can be clicked in the name field to sort in ascending or descending order and group by type e.g. clicking on file section will place all payroll files together, all general correspondence together etc.

When searching for saved documents, it is possible to apply filters based on time scales, as illustrated below, or based on the "folder" in which it was saved.

Date Range			
⦿ **Item Date**	○ **Item Received Date**		○ **Full Range**
○ Last Day	○ Last Week	○ Last Month	○ Last 3 Months
○ Last 6 Months	○ Last 12 Months	⦿ Last 18 Months	○ All
○ Others			

If no specific folder is chosen, all the data meeting that date or other criteria are displayed, but a summary of the numbers of documents in each folder are shown, and it is possible to drill down to any specific area simply by clicking on the name. We could click on the VAT tab as illustrated below and 7 documents would be displayed.

All	01. General Corres.(44)	02b. Tax: Corporate(1)	02c. VAT(7)	03. Accounts and Non Corp Working Papers 1)	05. Siç ‹

So how could *you* use document management and what difference might it make to your business?

Key questions and takeaways from the "Document management" section

Are we short of storage space, renting offsite storage, or could we make better use of storerooms? Will this be an issue at some stage in the future?	
Is it possible that multiple members of staff need access to the same customer/client files at the same time?	
Do we store files electronically and what system or methodology do we have in place?	
How long does it take to locate paper based files from around the office, or retrieve paper based files/folders from storage?	
Are emails and how they are handled/distributed an issue?	
What are our printing costs over the course of a year?	
What are our photocopying costs over the course of a year, and what happens to the photocopies?	
How do we know staff are "under pressure" and have backlogs of work piling up unactioned?	

Cloud vs On Premises Servers

If a one man band with only one person needing access to a PC and data, a single PC, often a laptop, is used. This generally contains all the programs and all the data relevant to the business. The use of cloud based software is increasing and this means the data is probably no longer stored on the PC. However, there are still many programs which do still reside on the PC along with the data.

What happens if the PC is lost? Or dropped? Or stolen? Or the hard disk fails? Whilst there may be backups, these may not be done as often as they should and it would still take some time to configure a new PC to get fully up and running again.

As the business grows, it becomes necessary to share data and a network needs to be set up. As this expands further, it becomes necessary to have a "server", in effect a PC to which all the other PCs in the office link to enable data sharing.

This server needs configuration in the first place and may require regular monitoring and attention - often bought in from IT suppliers. The PCs that are used in the business are often of quite a high specification in terms of memory, storage, and disk space and tend to need replacement on a fairly regular basis. There is also a considerable investment of time in unpacking a new PC from its box, configuring it to work on the server, installing all the necessary programs etc.

Another time consuming task with in house servers is the updating of software. When a new version or patch is issued, this needs to be updated locally on all of the PCs. This may happen automatically, or it may be necessary to wander round to all of the PCs and perform a manual installation.

There are however other options and becoming increasingly common is the hosted solution. My own business has been fully hosted for nearly 4 years (at the time of writing). In essence, all our data is held on a remote server in a "server farm", and we log in via the internet to use the programs. All processing is done remotely too. This means we have no servers at all in the office. The PCs we use to access the hosted desktop only need to be able to access the internet so we can use "thin client" devices - which are much cheaper than PCs to both purchase in the first place and to run in terms of electricity. In fact, we can access all programs and data from a mobile smartphone or tablets such as iPhones or iPads as well as Netbooks, Apple Macs etc.

There are other factors which can adversely affect access when data is on servers in the office. These are the natural disasters such as flooding or fire and adverse weather conditions such as snow. The data held on the remote server is also replicated in real time to another server farm in another area of the country, so I would contend our data is far more secure on the remote server than it was in the office.

The hosted route is suitable for any size of business - from the one man band upwards. If everything runs on the hosted server, if a PC fails, or is stolen, another PC can be purchased and the business can be up and running immediately.

Another advantage is the ability to access data from anywhere there is internet access. This could be at home, at a client or customer's premises, in a hotel or even sat on the beach.

Instead of capital expenditure every 5 years or so for a new server and replacing PCs, a monthly charge per user is paid. If a new staff member comes along, an email to the support staff is all that is required, and a login can be created quickly and easily-we need to give just 24 hours' notice. It is also scalable the other way and users can also be removed with 24 hours' notice. This makes it a very flexible proposition. Discounted pricing is also available for part time staff.

All software updates are performed by the hosted support staff, in our case out of normal office hours to minimise the downtime associated with this task.

Some users find that the hosted desktop environment is actually faster than their old systems due to the fact that enterprise grade, high performance servers and storage arrays are used in the data centres.

Key questions and takeaways from the "In house servers or a hosted solution?" section

How often do we replace PCs and at what cost?	
How often do we replace servers and at what cost?	
What specialist support do we need to maintain and keep our servers running?	
How long would it take to fully get up and running again in the event of a disaster - fire, flood etc.?	
Would access from anywhere be of benefit to us?	
How do we take backups at the present time, and have these been tested?	
Where are backups stored? Onsite? Offsite?	

A Miscellany of products and tools to boost efficiency

Here we pick up on various other hardware, software and working methods that can boost efficiencies and save valuable time.

Hardware

Multiple monitors

This has to rank as one of the best methods of improving efficiencies, and various studies over the years have proved this. One of the features of modern life is a plethora of different products used during the course of a working day. Some of the products, more often than not, are running at the same time, and it is common to have to take data from, or refer to data inside one product and use it in the other. This may be by simple copying and pasting, or it may be by transcribing or copying from one to the other.

A couple of simple examples;

- in the accountant's office, taking a Xero trial balance and inputting it into final accounts software. So there would be Xero open in one window, and final accounts software in another. On a large enough screen, it may be possible to display these windows side by side so that both are visible at the same time. It would be immensely time consuming and error prone to have to open one window, select a figure, then minimise that window, open the other one and input that information. So what happens? The data gets printed out and it is then keyed in from the printout.
- The email software is open all the time, as is the shared calendar. When an email comes in or someone phones up to make an appointment, the existing working window needs closing down or

minimising and the relevant software window needs to be opened or maximised.

- Payroll information has been scanned and is sat in the document management software and now needs to be entered into the payroll software.....you can hopefully see where this is going so there is no need to go into further detail on this example.

The solution? Multiple monitors.

Instead of having just one monitor attached to the PC, there are two....or three...or more...When buying new PCs ensure they have graphics cards that support at least two monitors. All is not lost however. You can buy graphics cards and insert into PCs. By far the easiest and quickest way of adding monitors though is to find a USB monitor. These plug into a USB port and no graphics card is required.

More than 50% of my office staff have three monitors on their desks. I was in a business in Scotland a little while ago where they were trialing the use of multiple monitors. I announced to one of the ladies that I had come to take away her second monitor as it was not proving successful.....and just about escaped alive from the building! You will not find anyone that goes back to using just a single monitor after having multiple screens. I have three on my desk at work and two at home. I also have a USB monitor that I can plug into a laptop when out and about or working on it at home.

Scanners

A scanner converts paper documents into electronic files. The electronic files can then be used in a variety of ways as we have seen. They can be forwarded to Receipt Bank or other software so that the data can be extracted into accounting software; they can be saved into Document Management systems or to Windows folders; they can be forwarded to others……

As with buying any hardware these days, there are always hundreds to choose from at a vast range of prices, and one that you can buy today could just as easily be a discontinued product tomorrow. You may already have scanning capabilities in the form of a multi-function device – combining fax, photocopier and scanner. This may be a heavy duty office wide device or it could be a cheap (under £100) inkjet printer/scanner/copier.

The cheap and cheerful printer may be sufficient for very occasional use, but we would not advocate it if you are going to be scanning regularly. They are generally flatbed scanners, scanning just one sheet at a time placed on the scanning bed. A sheet fed scanner is recommended.

Bearing in mind our proviso earlier about products being discontinued and a plethora of products out there, we will pick one that is available at the date of this publication.

The **Fujitsu ScanSnap iX500** is a simple solution for scanning and organising your files at the touch of a button. This scanner has a recommended throughput of up to 1,000 documents per day – which should be sufficient for many businesses. Scanning up to 50 pages per minute and offering resolutions of up to 1200dpi, Fujitsu's iX500 offers the perfect balance between efficiency and quality. It features smart phone (iOS and Android) connectivity and a standard version of Adobe Acrobat XI is also included in the price

To operate, simply place the sheets to be scanned into the automatic feeder, press SCAN and ScanSnap will:
• Scan both sides of the page
• Detect the size of the page
• Detect colour, grayscale or black and white
• Detect blank pages
• Detect page orientation
• Straighten skewed images
• Create fully searchable PDFs on Windows or Mac

The iX500 offers seamless linking to Cloud services allowing you to access your documents from any device, wherever and whenever you need it. The iX500 supports direct scanning to Evernote, Dropbox, Google Docs,

SalesForce and SugarSync. With built-in Wi-Fi, the iX500 offers the unique ability to link directly with mobile devices including iPad, iPhone and Android smartphones or tablets. Users can also wirelessly operate the scanner via their Smart Device and the ScanSnap Connect Application - creating high quality scanned images that can be saved to the device, manipulated, retrieved at a later date and distributed.

So this scanner could be used to scan invoices for instance to Drop Box and there is automatic integration between Drop Box and Receipt Bank so that the documents are taken into Receipt Bank at regular intervals and they will then automatically appear in your accounting records.

Link to Amazon

http://bit.ly/Scanix500

Software

A few software products and tips to make real world computing easier and more manageable.

Snipping Tool

In later versions of Windows there is a Snipping Tool, You can use Snipping Tool to capture a screen shot, or snip, of any object on your screen, and then annotate, save, or share the image. This tool will have been used to capture many of the images used in this publication.

You can capture any of the following types of snips:

- Free-form Snip. Draw a free-form shape around an object.

- Rectangular Snip. Drag the cursor around an object to form a rectangle.
- Window Snip. Select a window, such as a browser window or dialog box, that you want to capture.
- Full-screen Snip. Capture the entire screen.

After you capture a snip, it's automatically copied to the Clipboard and the mark-up window

You can access this by clicking on the Start button, All Programs, Accessories and the Snipping Tool, but this is quire laborious if you use it frequently.

It is suggested that you get to the above stage then right click on the Snipping Tool when highlighted and select "Pin to Taskbar". This icon will then appear on the taskbar at the foot of the screen ready for instant use.

If you want to capture a snip of a menu, such as the Start menu, follow these steps:

1. Open Snipping Tool by clicking the Start button ⬤. In the search box, type Snipping Tool, and then, in the list of results, click Snipping Tool.

2. After you open Snipping Tool, press Esc, and then open the menu that you want to capture.

3. Press Ctrl+PrtScn.

4. Click the arrow next to the New button, select Free-form Snip, Rectangular Snip, Window Snip, or Full-screen Snip from the list, and then select the area of your screen that you want to capture.

If someone has a query on any product encourage/train them to send a screenshot through as it will make it so much easier to see what they are talking about than trying to explain the issue either verbally or in an email.

To do Lists

How do you (and your staff) manage their tasks and things to do? Chances are many are using handwritten lists crossing them off as they get done, and then as they run out of space on the paper, rewrite on a clean sheet all the ones still left to do…. Sound familiar?

As highlighted throughout this publication there are always alternative solutions to a problem and this is no exception. Outlook is one tool which could be used. However, a free tool with paid for enhancements is toodledo (www.toodledo.com). This can run either in a web browser or be accessible via mobile devices such as smartphones or tablets.

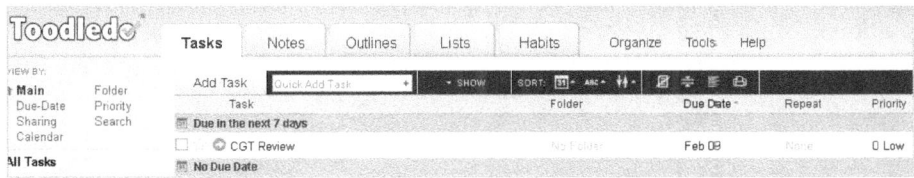

There is the option to list tasks, make notes, outlines, lists and habits. The to-do list can be organised into folders to keep track of different projects or work related tasks.

Collaboration is possible on paid for versions.

Password managers

How many logins and passwords do you have? Are you fortunate in having a photographic memory? Or do you need to have them written down somewhere? How do your staff maintain their own passwords?

A few ways this has been seen to be done:-

- Paper sticky note attached to the computer monitor (really!)
- Electronic sticky note on the Windows desktop
- Word document – called "passwords"
- Excel document – called "passwords"
- On a notepad in the desk drawer

Chances are high that the Word and/or Excel documents will be saved in an unprotected format with no password applied to them that need to be entered before opening. There is also a fair bet that the passwords will be insecure – e.g. password or 12345678.

Not only are there security issues, there can also be significant time wasted in keying in user logins and passwords. It may take 30-45 seconds to type in a lengthy email address as the login and then the 8-10 digit password. It will take considerably longer if the login is not used frequently and it needs to be looked up in one of the methods referred to above. The phrase "it does not take very long" springs to mind. Agreed 30-45 seconds is not long in isolation – but what if the login is entered 10-20 (or more) times a day-every day of every week?

Use of a password manager is recommended. As with everything we have considered in this publication there are always alternatives but Lastpass is one recommended. All the logins and passwords are saved into the Lastpass vault. Just one master password is required to be remembered to access this Lastpass vault. Once logged in, any website that is visited or any program that is launched can have the login and password completed automatically.

The vault is accessible on any device so it can be used on the home PC or laptop as well as the office PC. It can also be accessed via the website.

Web Browsers - Use the Toolbars for quick access to frequently accessed web pages

You can add web pages so that they automatically start up when your Internet Browser is opened. However you may have others that you use less frequently but still want rapid access to them when needed. You can add pages as bookmarks but this can be very time consuming to scroll down through a very long list.

In Firefox, there is a Bookmarks Toolbar which sits just under the main search box. Clicking on View – Toolbars and ensure Bookmarks Toolbar is ticked.

When a window is shown in the search box, this can be clicked and dragged to the Bookmarks Toolbar – ready for use as and when needed. Right click on the bookmarks and select Properties if you want to change the description etc.

You are able to do the same in both Chrome and Internet Explorer. For Internet Explorer click View – Toolbars and ensure the "favorites toolbar" is ticked.

In Chrome click on the customize button in the top right of the screen

 click on bookmarks and "Show bookmarks bar".

Printing Tools

There are a couple of printing tools that are invaluable.

PriPrinter

A favourite tool and the default "printer" in my own business. This is a printer driver that sits between the computer and the physical printer – a virtual printer. How many times do you send something to the printer and decide it is not correct or the layout is not right? You scrap the paper, amend your document and reprint it. Printing to PriPrinter lets you see the output on screen; if you are happy with it you can then send it to the physical printer. If there are issues you can either go back into the original application and change or there are many things you can do within PriPrinter itself.

You are able to delete or rearrange the pages, adjust margins, put many pages onto one sheet of paper, correct, remove or redact text, apply watermarks, change orientation, add page numbers etc.

Another major benefit is the ability to print from different products and then print the whole to one PDF file. You could print a profit and loss account and balance sheet from accounts software and then print graphs created in Excel and a report created in Word and combine them all together in one PDF file.

There is also the ability to create letterheads and forms. You can therefore create stationery and have this printed as part of the output.

PDF Creation software

PDF (Portable Document Format) is a file format used to present documents in a manner independent of the application software, hardware and operating systems. There are many software packages that you can download – some free, some paid for – to create PDF files. Some products have this functionality built in – e.g. when saving a document in later versions of Word there is an option to Create a PDF document.

We will mention just one in this publication – a free PDF software - CutePDF. There is also a Professional version which does require a payment and this adds lots more features to the basic free version.

Sharing a PDF file with someone means that as long as they have PDF Reader software on their device they should be able to view the document irrespective of whether they are looking at it on an iPad, iPhone, Apple Mac, Windows PC or indeed any other device.

PDF Reader and editor

Another essential in the armoury of business tools and highly recommended is PDF X-Change Viewer. As well as being a PDF Viewer it also allows you to manipulate the PDF Files. Some examples (this is not a comprehensive list);

- OCR (optical character recognition) can be run to make fully searchable files.

- Comments and annotations can be added (subject to security settings in the PDF file itself). So it is possible to type text onto a

PDF.

- Add and apply custom stamps. There are a range of stamps included which can be added to a PDF such as Draft, Confidential etc. However you can create your own from any image e.g. a signature can be created.

- Extract text from the pages

- Password protect PDF files so that a password is required to open them.

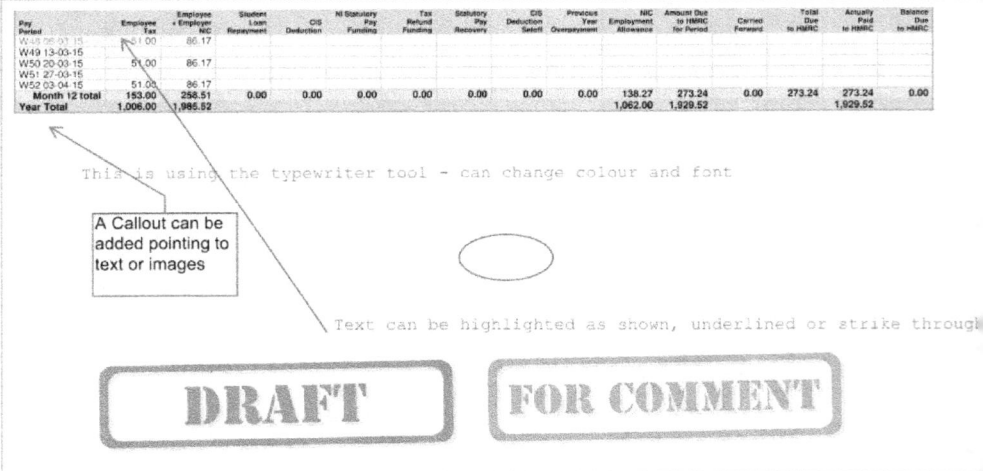

The use of electronic "sticky notes" can be used to pick out and highlight items in the main text. Indeed a proof of this publication was annotated in this way. Just one of the items highlighted is pictured below.

nd just about escaped
t monitor after having multiple
B monitor that I can plug into a

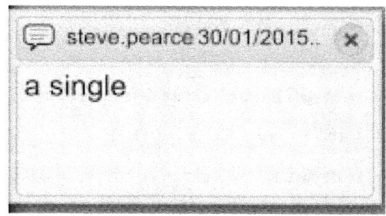

Moving to Xero

It is possible that other accounting software is already in use. However, there may be any number of reasons why it may be beneficial to make the transition to a different product. If the choice is made to move, the transition needs to be as painless as possible.

You may, by now, be thinking that you would really like to use Xero in your business and a key aim of this publication is to highlight tools and working methods to free up time and make processes more efficient.

The same principle applies in starting to use Xero as the accounting product of choice. The rekeying of data extracted from one product into Xero is not therefore an efficient method. Xero provides, via its help section, various files that can be downloaded and populated with data extracted from existing software or products assuming you can extract such information.

This allows the import of customer and supplier contacts, for example and fixed assets can also be imported.

However, there is a third party add-on, MoveMyBooks, which offers a fully managed service to convert data from Sage 50, Sage Instant Accounting, QuickBooks simple start, Standard, Pro or Premier. A backup of the existing data is uploaded to MoveMyBooks and within 3 days (and often very much sooner than that), the current year's transactions and the previous year's transactions can all be moved across, along with suppliers, customers etc. There is no need to wait until a financial year end has passed before thinking about or planning a transition. Having used this service on numerous occasions, it is highly recommended.

Video of the MoveMyBooks service

http://vimeo.com/68686175

Specific business and trade products linking to Xero

There are hundreds of products which link with Xero and new ones are being added all of the time. These are just a few selected to highlight the range of products using Xero as their preferred platform of choice. Note there are probably several other add-ons in the same category. These have been selected purely at random.

Don't see your type of business there? Visit the link below to explore further.

	Video link	Product links
Construction and Trades	http://geoop.com/quick-video-tutorials/	http://geoop.com/add-on-xero/
Farmers	http://vimeo.com/11489 2414	http://farmflo.com/
Healthcare		https://www.cliniko.com/xero
Automotive	http://youtu.be/m7Ck-yPPuPk	http://workshopsoftware.com.au/xero-integration/
Retail	http://youtu.be/JYPxnic1 1WE	http://www.unleashedsoftware.com/our-product/who-we-integrate-with/xero-inventory
Property Management		http://www.re-leased.com/
Vets		http://www.ezyvet.com/xero-accounting/
Law Firms	http://vimeo.com/80849 419	http://landing.goclio.com/xero/

You can review a comprehensive list of add-ons at the Xero website:-

https://www.xero.com/uk/add-ons/

Why not outsource all of your accounting function?

What is outsourcing? Wikipedia defines this as the contracting out of a business process to another party. Your business may well have done this in the past although not calling it outsourcing. Common outsourced business tasks include the payroll function and the preparation and submission of VAT returns. In the hands of those that now do this work, this is termed insourcing.

Why have these tasks been outsourced? There are many reasons:-

- a lack of time/resources
- a lack of expertise
- in-house staffing issues
- privacy of information and data security
- cost effectiveness

With the use of some or all of the technologies covered in this publication, it is now easier than ever to find someone prepared to insource all of your accounting functions. It is no longer necessary for someone to turn up in your factory or offices on a regular basis and sit there ploughing through paperwork. This can be done by someone working in an office anywhere in the world, working at home or even sitting on a beach or by the pool!

Do you still have employees whose sole task is to maintain the purchase ledger – posting invoices and payments? What happens when they go off sick or on holiday? What happens when they leave? What happens when your business expands and they feel they need an assistant employed to help them? It is possible that your accountants may now be able to offer a cost effective and efficient solution to process the purchase ledger. With the use of the Credec payments via BACS there is the ability to outsource your payments too – you still have complete control over approval of the payments entered.

But why just purchase ledger? Your bookkeeper may have moved on elsewhere. Why not consider the outsourcing next time you need help?

Keys to ensuring this is successful

- Ensure that as much information as possible is made available to those now doing the work for you. They cannot "guess" what a cheque is for or who the payee is; likewise they need to know whether a receipt is for sales or perhaps own funds introduced into the business.
- Ensure information is supplied in a timely manner especially where there are deadlines to be met such as VAT returns.
- Respond to queries raised promptly too!
- Supplier statements are also needed to ensure that all invoices have been picked up. Don't just throw them away or assume they are not required.
- Ensure automated bank and other feeds are activated.

So how will "doing the accounts" change for you?

We considered at the beginning the "standard" and long established methodologies for accounting and record keeping. Throughout we have challenged those methods and suggested alternative ways. Before we finish, let's take a final look at a scenario that is achievable and is working now for many businesses.

Consider for a minute what is perhaps the ultimate in bookkeeping. It won't work for all businesses but there will be a few where this is not "pie in the sky" and can be implemented.

Invoices are sent out regularly (monthly or quarterly) to selected customers in respect of a service. These invoices can be set up as recurring invoices in Xero and these can be set to be emailed out automatically as soon as they are raised. One of the add-on products interrogates the debtors ledger on a regular basis, identifies when the invoice is due for payment and automatically collects this sum on the due date by direct debit. The funds are collected from the customer's bank account and paid directly into your own bank account. This sum is then automatically marked as paid in Xero, and the charges associated with this collection are posted into the relevant expense account. When the transaction appears in the bank it is imported into the bank account via the automated bank feed.

So the whole of the accounting transaction has been entered into the records without any manual intervention whatsoever!

Are you still going to do what you have always done, or are you going to make changes – or at least investigate further? It is sincerely hoped that this publication does encourage you to take action.

Xero accounting software has been the biggest driver in moving the goalposts and here are a few reasons.

Why do people love Xero?

- Automated daily bank feeds
- Bank reconciliation
- Fast, simple and customised invoicing
- VAT reporting and reconciliations
- Available anytime, anywhere you're online
- Real time collaboration with your professional advisers
- Safe and secure
- Smart reports with links to source transactions
- Budgets and variance reporting
- Expense claims
- Fixed assets
- Multi-currency
- Dashboard gives a clear financial overview
- Awesome support at no additional cost
- No installation or IT maintenance required
- Pay as you go and no up-front costs

The next steps...?

There are various links to videos and other resources throughout this publication, and there are hundreds more available if you search for them.

As a certified Xero partner we work with many businesses using both Xero and a range of add-ons. With our IT knowledge and credentials we have worked with a number of the add-on partners in the development, testing and feedback.

The ICAEW run an "accredited products" scheme and Xero has been through the accreditation process, which has been carried out by Glover Stanbury & Co partner, Kevin Salter on behalf of the ICAEW.

Xero run their own certification process and certain of our support staff complete this annually to ensure we are fully up to date.

It does not matter where you are – we can help you and work with you. Whilst our offices are in north Devon, we have clients using Xero all over the UK, and also as far afield as the USA, Spain and Poland.

Give us a call or drop us an email – find us at www.gloverstanbury.co.uk

www.ingramcontent.com/pod-product-compliance
Lightning Source LLC
Chambersburg PA
CBHW070231210526
45168CB00020B/1925